THE POWER OF RELIGION
IN THE PUBLIC SPHERE

The POWER *of* RELIGION *in the* PUBLIC SPHERE

JUDITH BUTLER
JÜRGEN HABERMAS
CHARLES TAYLOR
CORNEL WEST

Edited and introduced by

Eduardo Mendieta and Jonathan VanAntwerpen

Afterword by Craig Calhoun

COLUMBIA UNIVERSITY PRESS

A COLUMBIA / SSRC BOOK

NEW YORK

Columbia University Press
Publishers Since 1893
New York Chichester, West Sussex
Copyright © 2011 The Social Science Research Council
All rights reserved
Library of Congress Cataloging-in-Publication Data

The power of religion in the public sphere / Judith Butler . . . [et al.]; edited
with an introduction by Eduardo Mendieta and Jonathan VanAntwerpen;
with an afterword by Craig Calhoun.
   p. cm.
   Includes bibliographical references.
   ISBN 978-0-231-15645-5 (cloth: alk. paper) —ISBN 978-0-231-15646-2
(pbk.: alk. paper)
   1. Civil religion. 2. Religion and state. 3. Religion and politics.
I. Butler, Judith, 1956– II. Mendieta, Eduardo. III. VanAntwerpen,
Jonathan, 1970– IV. Title.
  BL98.5.P69 2011
   201'.72—dc22

2010028751

CONTENTS

Acknowledgments VII

Introduction: *The Power of Religion in the Public Sphere*
EDUARDO MENDIETA AND JONATHAN VANANTWERPEN I

"The Political": *The Rational Meaning of a Questionable
Inheritance of Political Theology*
JÜRGEN HABERMAS 15

Why We Need a Radical Redefinition of Secularism
CHARLES TAYLOR 34

Dialogue: *Jürgen Habermas and Charles Taylor* 60

Is Judaism Zionism?
JUDITH BUTLER 70

CONTENTS

Prophetic Religion and the Future of Capitalist Civilization
CORNEL WEST   92

Dialogue: *Judith Butler and Cornel West*   101

Concluding Discussion: *Butler, Habermas, Taylor, West*   109

Afterword: *Religion's Many Powers*
CRAIG CALHOUN   118

Index   135

ACKNOWLEDGMENTS

This volume is the result of an event that was jointly sponsored by three different institutions, with particular support and encouragement from a number of individuals. Abbreviated versions of the essays published here were first presented at a public event in the historic Great Hall of New York City's Cooper Union. Held October 22, 2009, the event was cosponsored by New York University's Institute for Public Knowledge, the Social Science Research Council, and Stony Brook University. Over a thousand people converged, queuing around the block and eventually packing the Great Hall to listen to Judith Butler, Jürgen Habermas, Charles Taylor, and Cornel West hold forth and engage with one another for almost five hours. In addition to this volume's four main chapters, edited transcripts of dialogues between the authors are also reproduced here, interwoven between individual contributions, as they were at the event itself. Craig Calhoun, our co-organizer for the event, generously agreed to write an afterword.

We are especially grateful to our four authors for their participation in the public dialogue and for graciously writing and then editing their texts and reviewing the transcripts of their extemporaneous remarks. Without their willingness, generosity, and temerity, this book would not have been possible. We are also indebted to Craig Calhoun, who arranged financial support for the public dialogue, and to Robert Crease, Eric Kaler, and Nancy Squires at Stony Brook University, who provided additional support and encouragement. We owe special thanks to Ruth Braunstein, Samuel Carter, and Evan Ray of NYU (for assistance in organizing the event); to Paul Price, Charles Gelman, and Jessica Polebaum of the SSRC (for assistance with manuscript preparation and help with other details); to Matthias Fritsch, María Herrera Lima, David Kyuman Kim, and Max Pensky (for timely and helpful comments on an earlier version of our introduction); and to Wendy Lochner of Columbia University Press (who made the volume's publication an editorial priority). We are, above all, thankful to the more than one thousand individuals who participated in a long and undeniably epic event. This book is a testament to the vitality of the public sphere, in its uniquely American incarnation.

THE POWER OF RELIGION
IN THE PUBLIC SPHERE

INTRODUCTION

The Power of Religion in the Public Sphere

EDUARDO MENDIETA AND JONATHAN VANANTWERPEN

Many of our dominant stories about religion and public life are myths that bear little relation to either our political life or our everyday experience. Religion is neither merely private, for instance, nor purely irrational. And the public sphere is neither a realm of straightforward rational deliberation nor a smooth space of unforced assent. Yet these understandings of both religion and public life have long been pervasive, perhaps especially within academic circles. In recent years, however, and in the midst of a widespread resurgence of interest in the public importance of religion, there has been an increasingly sophisticated series of intellectual interventions challenging us to reconsider our most basic categories of research, analysis, and critique. Just as, in an earlier period, feminists and other scholars raised fundamental questions about the meaning of the public and its relation to the private, today the very categories of the religious and the secular—and of secularism and religion—are being revisited, reworked, and rethought.[1]

Such rethinking, we believe, represents a significant moment of opportunity. With this in mind, we invited four prominent public philosophers—Judith Butler, Jürgen Habermas, Charles Taylor, and Cornel West—to take part in a dialogue on "the power of religion in the public sphere." This book represents the remarkable response from these important thinkers. In this volume, as in the public event that inspired it, these four intellectuals address both one another and a broader public, each taking up a different strand of the complicated engagement between religion and the public sphere. Each of our contributors is a highly respected scholar and a well-known public intellectual. Each is a philosopher, though all have moved well beyond the academic discipline of philosophy. Each has a distinctive intellectual style, a particular philosophical project, a wide interdisciplinary reach, and a strong commitment to public engagement. Together they represent some of the most influential and original philosophical voices writing today, spanning the spectrum of critical theory in its latest forms, from pragmatism and poststructuralism to feminist theory and critical race theory, hermeneutics, phenomenology, the philosophy of language, and beyond. Through their individual essays, as well as in their dialogues with one another, they provide us with fresh takes on what has been for each of them an abiding concern with the place of religion in the public sphere.

The study of the public sphere was pioneered in a provocative and incisive way by Jürgen Habermas's *The Structural Transformation of the Public Sphere,* and contemporary discussions of the "public" and related categories remain closely linked to this genealogical work, crafted more than forty years ago and translated into English in the late 1980s.[2] The book offered a historical reconstruction of the emergence, growth, and eventual decline of the bourgeois public sphere, aiming to elucidate its normative dimensions and to distill an ideal type. The public sphere that began to emerge in the eighteenth century, according to Habermas, developed as a social space—distinct from the state, the economy, and the family—in which individuals could engage each other as private citizens deliberating about the common good. Perhaps the most crucial aspect of this new social structure was its status as a space of reason-giving, a realm in which reasons were forwarded and debated, accepted or rejected. Nominally, the public sphere was an indefinitely open space in which all reasons could be expressed and heard. Only those arguments and reasons would be accepted that could meet the assent of all participants. In this way, while the state monopolized coercion, the public sphere became the social space in which all force was transformed into the coercion of rational deliberation—what Habermas would later develop as the "unforced force" of the better argument. At the same time, inasmuch as the bourgeois public sphere became an ideal that was never completely actualized, it turned into an unremitting self-critique of modern society that simultaneously called forth greater scrutiny of the "public sphere" itself.

As critics of *The Structural Transformation* have pointed out, Habermas paid insufficient attention to religion in this early work. Indeed, in his introduction to an influential collection on *Habermas and the Public Sphere*, Craig Calhoun noted not only Habermas's relative "neglect of religion" but also—and more forcefully—his "antireligious assumptions."[3] Yet, in the last several years, Habermas has turned increasingly to questions of religion.[4] His contribution here, which opens the volume, builds on and goes beyond these recent interventions.[5] Closely considering the problematic and ambivalent notion of "the political"—associated in particular with the work of both Carl Schmitt and Leo Strauss—Habermas criticizes Schmitt's "clerico-fascist" conception of the political as the binding source for all authority and opposes himself to recent attempts to revive political theology. He argues, instead, that the "religiously connotated concept" of the political must be historicized, since it corresponds to an earlier stage in the evolution of human society, a time when the power of the state was guaranteed by a mythological-religious worldview. The political, Habermas suggests, represents the image of society as a totality and the "symbolic field in which the early civilizations first formed an image of themselves." Today, however, this conception of the political has become not just anachronistic but regressive. The political system has been submitted to the demystifying power of deliberation in the public sphere. Indeed, society can no longer be understood as a totality precisely because its self-representations are now plural, contested, and contestable.

What, then, explains the recent and full-throated return of political theology, with its central and seemingly anachronistic concept of "the political"? Here Habermas points to the experience of contemporary world society as a juggernaut driven by intractable economic forces seemingly beyond human control. Against the technological, economic, and cultural chaos of a world integrated into one gigantic structure, the image of "the political" promises to return control to human agents. Contemporary political theology offers the hope of substantive politics, over and against a widely prevailing view that sees citizens merely as clients or pawns, caught within a society shorn of political self-determination. Yet such promises are both illusory and dangerous, Habermas suggests, for they presuppose a return to a period prior to the domestication of state power by both law and the public sphere. Against attempts to revive political theology, Habermas juxtaposes John Rawls's approach to religion in the public sphere. He is both critical and appreciative of the work of Rawls, who emerges here as the paragon of the view that we cannot confuse the secularization of the state with the secularization of society.

In recognition of the fact that religion has not withered away under the pressures of modernization, Habermas has increasingly stressed the importance of cultivating a "postsecular" stance, an approach that both reckons with the continuing global vitality of religion and emphasizes the importance of "translating" the ethical insights of religious traditions with a view to their incorporation into a "postmetaphysical" philosophical perspective. The postsecular stance looks to religious sources of meaning and motivation as both a helpful and even indispensable ally in confronting the forces of global capitalism, while underscoring the crucial difference between faith and knowledge.[6] Religious practices and perspectives, Habermas concludes, continue to be key sources of the values that nourish an ethics of multicultural citizenship, commanding both solidarity and equal respect. Yet, in order for the "vital semantic potentials from religious traditions" to be made available for wider political culture (and, in particular, within democratic institutions), they must be translated into a secular idiom and a "universally accessible language," a task that falls not only to religious citizens but to all citizens—both religious and secular—engaged in the public use of reason.

In the following chapter, Charles Taylor takes issue with this conception of public reason and aims to unsettle the ways in which we have conceived secularism. While Habermas is severely critical of recent attempts to renew the concept of "the political," and seems to think that modern secular states might do altogether without some analogous concept, Taylor suggests otherwise. Democratic societies, he argues, remain organized around a strong "philosophy of civility," a normative conception linked to what he has called the "modern moral order."

The rise and shape of this conception of the modern moral order is something that Taylor has explored in substantial depth in recent work, first in a relatively short volume entitled *Modern Social Imaginaries* and subsequently in his monumental *A Secular Age*.[7] Modern social imaginaries, he has suggested, both inform and are informed by the modern moral order, and they represent "not a set of ideas" but rather "what enables, through making sense of, the practices of a society."[8] Along with markets and democratic citizenship, the conception of the "public sphere" mobilizes one such imaginary, offering a vision of social order as produced by the individual actions of strangers, both reflecting and reproducing crucial aspects of modern social life.

Modern democratic societies, then, are organized around new understandings of order, including those embedded within conceptions of the public sphere—and in this sense they are organized around a new conception of "the political." Yet diverse democracies nonetheless cannot revert to a full-blown shared conception of social and political life, but are rather constrained to pursue what Rawls called an "overlapping consensus." In pursuit of such consensus, what role should religious reasons play? Here too Taylor parts ways to a certain extent with Habermas. Calling for a "radical redefinition of secularism," and critically considering an enduring "fixation on religion"—a misguided emphasis on religion's uniqueness that, he suggests, Habermas shares with Rawls and a range of other political philosophers—Taylor argues that religion's place in the public sphere should not be taken as a "special case," though, for a range of historical reasons, it has come to be seen as such.

The idea that secularism ought to treat religion as a special case, Taylor suggests, derives in good part from the history of secularism in the West, and especially its emergence in the two important "founding contexts" of the United States and France, in which Christianity loomed large (albeit in different ways in each case). The continuing fixation on religion, he argues, also has deeper epistemological roots in an enduring "myth" of the Enlightenment, a myth that sets apart nonreligiously informed reason—"reason alone"—as deserving a special and privileged status, while conceiving of religiously based conclusions as "dubious, and in the end only convincing to people who have already accepted the dogmas in question." This distinction, which emerges in the work of Habermas in the form of an "epistemic break" between secular reason and religious thought, is ultimately untenable, Taylor suggests, since the notion of state neutrality that motivates secularism is a response to the diversity not just of religious positions but of nonreligious positions as well. There is no reason to single out religion, Taylor argues, as against nonreligious viewpoints.

In place of an understanding of secularism that fixes on religion as the central problem, Taylor offers instead an alternative conception understood in terms of the balancing or coordinating of the claims of different goods that democratic societies take to be fundamental. He suggests that we can understand these fundamental goods in terms of many different expansions or readings of the three professed values of the French revolution: liberty, equality, and fraternity. Outlining a "revisionary polysemy" that places central emphasis on the attempt to secure these primary social goods, Taylor concludes that regimes deserving of the label *secularist* be conceived not primarily as "bulwarks against religion" but rather as those that respond in a principled fashion to the irreversible and ever growing internal diversity of modern societies. Appropriate responses to such diversity, all of which should seek to maximize the basic goals of liberty and equality between basic beliefs, are bound to be context specific, and there is no algorithm that can determine the shape of a particular secular regime. In many Western countries, where secularism initially emerged as a vehicle for protecting against some form or other of religious domination, there has subsequently been a shift toward a more widespread diversity of basic beliefs—religious, nonreligious, and areligious. In these contexts, as in others, Taylor argues, there is a need to balance freedom of conscience and equality of respect, in particular so as not to needlessly limit the religious freedoms of immigrant minorities whose religious practices have in some cases been taken to violate historically established secular norms and institutional arrangements.

Judith Butler's contribution follows, after a short dialogue between Habermas and Taylor. If Habermas and Taylor offer sociotheoretical genealogies and hermeneutic narratives of the public sphere, Butler provides what we might call a syntax of the public. In her most explicit contribution to a political theory of the public, *Excitable Speech: A Politics of the Performative*, Butler explored what it means that we are "beings who require language in order to be."[9] A central chapter of the book, on "linguistic vulnerability," considered the "ritual of interpellation" by means of which social agents are called into being—named, addressed, and ushered into a subject position. As we are brought into social existence, Butler argues, there is no way to foreclose the possibility of being interpellated in injurious, disquieting, and unsettling ways.[10] Indeed, to be a subject of speech is precisely to always be open to such unexpected interpellations. This radical vulnerability has evident political consequences. At the very least, it makes explicit under what conditions politics is possible. A politics that refuses and neglects this linguistic vulnerability, Butler argues, extinguishes the prerogative of agency itself as a political task. Politics is a response to the risk that the foundational injurability of agency entails.

Butler's contribution to the present volume once again takes up the question of politics, public speech, and vulnerability. It can be read, in a sense, as making good on a promissory note in an argument she made in an essay that first appeared in the *London Review of Books* under the title "No, It's Not Anti-Semitic."[11] In this powerful text, Butler confronted a public strategy that seeks to control a particular kind of speech that circulates in the public sphere—"to terrorize with the charge of anti-Semitism, and to produce a climate of fear through the use of a heinous judgment with which no progressive person would want to identify."[12] Against this strategy, she juxtaposed another ethos, one that made speaking against illegitimate state violence imperative, even if it "poses a risk to ourselves."[13] In her essay here, Butler further develops this ethos, showing how it is related to both vulnerability and injurability.

The essay opens with a series of incisive remarks that starkly profile the aims of the entire book. Calling attention to the plurality of religious conceptions of public life, Butler suggests that the public sphere is itself an effect of certain religious traditions, which "help to establish a set of criteria that delimit the public from the private." As such, secularization may not spell the demise of religion but, in fact, "may be a fugitive way for religion to survive." These challenging and instructive remarks then open out into a much more specific quandary: the tension that emerges between religion and public life when public criticism of Israeli state violence is taken to be anti-Semitic or anti-Jewish, and when—at the same time—to openly and publicly criticize state violence is in some ways an obligatory ethical demand from within both religious and nonreligious Jewish frameworks.

With this particular ethical demand in view, Butler sets out to delineate a Jewish ethos of exile and dispossession, at the core of which is the conception of co-habitation. To have been permanently rendered a refugee, she argues, is to always face the precariousness of one's habitation. It is then that the truth of the human condition flashes up, namely, that all habitation is always cohabitation and always fragile. Drawing on diasporic traditions within Judaism in order to reanimate an ideal of co-habitation, Butler stresses both its value and its unavoidability. "To co-habit is prior to any possible community or nation or neighborhood," she writes. "We might choose where to live, and who to live by, but we cannot choose with whom to co-habit the earth." To seek to decide with whom to cohabit, then, is to seek to preempt a basic condition of social and political existence. Rather, Butler argues, we must actively seek to preserve "the non-chosen character of inclusive and plural co-habitation." As such, the ideal—and the basic reality—of co-habitation both forms the ethical basis for public critique of Israeli state violence and represents the other side of the fundamental dispossession that is the mark of vulnerable and injurable agency. It may not be inaccurate to suggest that the public sphere—constituted as it is by "limits on the audible and the sensible" and by exclusions of various kinds—is precisely that place where we jointly face the risk of dispossession, vulnerability, and injurability. Further, this insight into human fragility was elaborated and preserved by a group of thinkers whose religious and ethnic identity were both enabled and dispossessed by modalities of the public sphere.

The last of the four main essays in this book is by a public intellectual and cultural critic who has both shaped and been shaped by the public sphere, Cornel West. At the beginning of our public event, Habermas referred to West as an ideal dialogue partner. Indeed, West has transformed the meaning of "public" in public intellectual, in his role as a cultural icon, a spoken-word philosopher, and—as he puts it—"a blues man in the life of the mind, a jazz man in the world of ideas." If Socrates had been born in the *fin de siècle* United States, it is perhaps not too much to suggest that he would have engaged publically much as West does—as a gadfly, a philosophical provocateur, and an intellectual midwife. West's repeated interventions within the American public sphere and beyond have consistently urged his listeners to take seriously the prophetic dimension of religiosity, while also engaging in a positive but critical evaluation of the achievements of American democracy. His contribution to our public forum was no exception, and we reproduce it here with only minor editorial revisions.

West's voice has been distinctive within American public life. His work is unapologetically socialist, Christian, and philosophical. He has called his brand of historical materialism, hermeneutical historicism, socialist democracy, black prophetic Christocentric religiosity, tragic existentialism, and democratic pragmatism "prophetic pragmatism."[14] Notwithstanding the ecumenical breadth and prodigious wealth of sources that inform his thinking, we may identify four central pillars in his philosophical-religious approach. The first is a distinct brand of prophetic Christianity, one that has taken shape through the Afro-American experience. The second is a historical materialist analysis of social exploitation, linking racial, gender, and class exploitation. The third is an appropriation and transformation of the American pragmatist tradition, with its focus on democratic determination and social melioration. And, finally, there is West's own distinct form of existentialist humanism tempered by recognition of the tragicomic in human life.[15]

In recent years, West has continued to stress the prophetic, Christocentric, and tragicomic dimension of his prophetic approach, emphasizing that the Christian tradition provides an existential insight into the "crises and traumas of life" that allows one to "hold at bay the sheer absurdity so evident in life, without erasing or eliding the tragedy of life."[16] As he puts it, "the culture of the wretched of the earth is deeply religious. To be in solidarity with them requires not only an acknowledgement of what they are up against but also an appreciation of how they cope with their situation. This appreciation does not require that one be religious; but if one is religious, one has wider access into their life-world."[17] It is for this reason that West has taken a critical stance vis-à-vis two prominent American defenders of political liberalism, John Rawls and Richard Rorty, criticizing both for adopting a dogmatic secularism that polices the public sphere and thereby depletes it of potentially enlightened voices. "Ought we not be concerned," he asks, "with the forms of dogmatism and authoritarianism in secular garb that trump dialogue and foreclose debate? Democratic practices—dialogue and debate in public discourse—are always messy and impure. And secular policing can be as arrogant and coercive as religious policing."[18]

West's contribution exemplifies precisely this call, reminding us of the importance of being "open to different discourses, arguments, pushing you against the wall." Secular thinkers, he argues, "must become more religiously musical," just as we all must seek to "broaden the scope of empathy and imagination, both in dialogue between secular brothers and sisters—atheistic, agnostic—and religious brothers and sisters." What makes his contribution both distinct and powerful is that West here embodies the power of the religious voice in the public sphere. Rather than offering a philosophical text, a social-analytical commentary, or even a hermeneutical reconstruction, West performs a vigorous and virtuosic translation among those traditions and languages that give substance and thickness to the public sphere. Syncopating, and riffing on philosophy and poetry, scripture and song, West makes a moving call to recognize the power of religion in our midst. This power emanates from distinctive religious traditions that serve as reservoirs of cultural memory as well as compendiums of utopian yearnings. Religious perspectives, West suggests, offering up the "prophetic twist," provide distinctive moral visions, compasses to track human misery and despair in our world, and "an empathetic and imaginative power that confronts hegemonic powers always operating."

Following West's contribution, a short dialogue between Butler and West, and a concluding discussion between all four authors, we close with an afterword by Craig Calhoun, moderator of that discussion and our co-organizer for the public event that inspired this book. President of the Social Science Research Council in New York City, and the director of the Institute for Public Knowledge at New York University, Calhoun is an internationally renowned interdisciplinary scholar, a leading thinker in American discussions of the public sphere, and an astute observer of religion. In his afterword he discusses the specific place of religion in the American public sphere before moving to a brief and incisive consideration of each of the four preceding chapters. His perspective is at once historical and theoretical. While the public prominence of religion, he writes, still has the capacity to startle secular thinkers, religion has in fact long been an important feature of American public life, even as the debates it arouses have regularly been the source of both confusion and struggle. Indeed, by weaving a rich historical and transcultural narrative about the ceaseless contributions of religion to contemporary cultural, political, social, and philosophical debates and movements, Calhoun illustrates an at times productive dialectic between secularization and religious vitality. The complex and contradictory vitality of religion, Calhoun concludes, cannot be—and perhaps should not be—easily absorbed into the public sphere. Yet, whether it figures as threat or inspiration, unreflective conviction or prophetic challenge, the power of religion in the public sphere demands and deserves our critical attention.

NOTES

1. See Craig Calhoun, Mark Juergensmeyer, and Jonathan VanAntwerpen, *Rethinking Secularism* (New York: Oxford University Press, forthcoming).

2. Jürgen Habermas, *The Structural Transformation of the Public Sphere: An Inquiry Into a Category of Bourgeois Society*, trans. Thomas Burger, with the assistance of Frederick Lawrence (Cambridge: MIT Press, 1989). Many of Habermas's subsequent theoretical proposals were either

first articulated in this book or resulted from tensions and contradictions first discerned within it.

3. See Craig Calhoun, "Introduction" in Craig Calhoun, ed., *Habermas and the Public Sphere* (Cambridge: MIT Press, 1992), pp. 35–36. See also the chapters by Keith Michael Baker, David Zaret, and Lloyd Kramer. Habermas subsequently acknowledged that a revised version of the book would have to give greater attention to the way in which the emergence of the bourgeois public sphere was indeed conditioned by religion. See his "Further Reflections on the Public Sphere" and "Concluding Remarks," ibid.

4. See Eduardo Mendieta, *Global Fragments: Globalizations, Latinamericanisms, and Critical Theory* (Albany: SUNY Press, 2007), chapter 8: "The Linguistification of the Sacred as a Catalyst of Modernity: Jürgen Habermas on Religion." See also Jürgen Habermas, in Eduardo Mendieta, ed., *Religion and Rationality: Essays on Reason, God, and Modernity* (Cambridge: Polity, 2002).

5. These include two recent interventions of particular note: a dialogue with then Cardinal Joseph Ratzinger (now Pope Benedict XVI) and an extended engagement with the work of political philosopher John Rawls. Both these texts are now in Jürgen Habermas, *Between Naturalism and Religion*, trans. Ciaran Cronin (Cambridge: Polity, 2008).

6. See Eduardo Mendieta, A Postsecular World Society? An Interview with Jürgen Habermas, The Immanent Frame, http://blogs.ssrc.org/tif/2010/02/03/a-postsecular-world-society/ (accessed March 1, 2010).

7. Charles Taylor, *Modern Social Imaginaries* (Durham: Duke University Press, 2004), *A Secular Age* (Cambridge: Harvard University Press, 2007).

8. Taylor, *Modern Social Imaginaries*, p. 2.

9. Judith Butler, *Excitable Speech: A Politics of the Performative* (New York: Routledge, 1997).

10. As Butler puts it: "There is no way to protect against the primary vulnerability and susceptibility to the call of recognition that solicits existence, to that primary dependency on a language we never made in order to acquire a tentative ontological status. . . . The address that inaugurates the possibility of agency, in a single stroke, forecloses the possibility of radical autonomy" (ibid., p. 26).

11. This essay was later published as "The Charge of Anti-Semitism: Jews, Israel, and the Risks of Public Critique," in Judith Butler, *Precarious*

Life: The Powers of Mourning and Violence (New York: Verso, 2004), pp. 101–127.

12. Ibid., pp. 120–121.

13. Ibid., p. 103.

14. See Cornel West, *The American Evasion of Philosophy: A Genealogy of Pragmatism* (Madison: University of Wisconsin Press, 1989), chapter 6: "Prophetic Pragmatism: Cultural Criticism and Political Engagement"; see also *Prophesy Deliverance! An Afro-American Revolutionary Christianity* (Philadelphia: Westminster, 1982), especially chapter 5: "Afro-American Revolutionary Christianity."

15. See Mendieta, *Global Fragments*, chapter 9: "Which Pragmatism? Whose America? On Cornel West."

16. West, *The American Evasion of Philosophy*, p. 233.

17. Ibid.

18. Cornel West, *Democracy Matters: Winning the Fight Against Imperialism* (New York: Penguin, 2004), p. 161.

"THE POLITICAL"

The Rational Meaning of a Questionable Inheritance of Political Theology

JÜRGEN HABERMAS

In the welfare state democracies of the latter half of the twentieth century, politics was still able to wield a steering influence on the diverging subsystems; it could still counterbalance tendencies toward social disintegration. Thus under the conditions of "embedded capitalism," politics could succeed in this effort *within the framework of the nation state.* Today, under conditions of globalized capitalism, the political capacities for protecting social integration are becoming dangerously restricted. As economic globalization progresses, the picture that systems theory sketched of social modernization is acquiring ever sharper contours in reality.

According to this interpretation, politics as a means of democratic self-determination has become as impossible as it is superfluous. Autopoietic functional subsystems conform to logics of their own; they constitute environments for one another, and have long since become independent from the undercomplex networks of the various lifeworlds of the population. "The political" has been transformed into the code of a self-maintaining administrative subsystem, so that democracy is in danger of becoming a mere facade, which the executive agencies turn toward their helpless clients. Systems integration responds to functional imperatives and leaves *social* integration behind as a far too cumbersome mechanism. Because the latter still proceeds via the minds of actors, its operation would have to rely upon the normative structures of lifeworlds that are, however, more and more marginalized.

Under the constraint of economic imperatives that increasingly hold sway over private spheres of life, individuals, intimidated, withdraw more and more into the bubble of their private interests. Willingness to engage in collective action, the awareness that citizens can at all collectively shape the social conditions of their lives through solidaristic action, fades under the perceived force of systemic imperatives. More than anything else, the erosion of confidence in the power of collective action and the atrophy of normative sensibilities reinforce an already smoldering skepticism with regard to an enlightened self-understanding of modernity. Hence the imminent danger of democracy becoming an "obsolete model" (Lutz Wingert) is the challenge that lends the apparently antiquated concept of "the political" new topicality.

At least for some contemporary French and Italian philosophers, in the tradition of Carl Schmitt, Leo Strauss, and Hannah Arendt, and for some students of Jacques Derrida, the classical concept of "the political" serves as an antidote against those depoliticizing tendencies of the age (let me only mention Ernesto Laclau, Giorgio Agamben, Claude Lefort, and Jean-Luc Nancy).[1] These colleagues extend their political reasoning to metaphysical and religious domains, which seem to transcend the trivial kind of administrative and power wrestling politics as we know it. Claude Lefort appeals to the difference between *le politique* (the political) and *la politique* (politics) in order to make us aware "that any society which forgets it religious basis is laboring under the illusion of pure self-immanence."[2]

I share Lefort's intention, but I think that the era when philosophy could elevate itself above the other disciplines belongs to the past. Today the social sciences lay claim to the political system as their subject matter; they deal with "politics," that is, with the struggle for and the exercise of power, and also with "policies"—that is, the goals and strategies pursued by political actors in different political fields. Besides normative political theory, philosophers have long since lost their special competence for the "political system." "The political" no longer appears to constitute a serious philosophical topic alongside "politics" and "policies." Yet there is reason to doubt whether the Enlightenment traditions can still generate sufficient motivations and social movements for preserving the normative contents of modernity out of its own resources. It is this doubt that lead me to ask whether we can give a rational meaning to the ambivalent concept of "the political." Let me first check a purely descriptive use of the term: From an empirical point of view, "the political" at best designates that symbolic field in which the early civilizations first formed an image of themselves.

1. From a historical point of view, "the political" leads us back to the origins of state-organized societies, such as the ancient empires of Mesopotamia, Syria, and Egypt, in which social integration had been partly transferred from kinship structure to the hierarchical form of royal bureaucracies. The emergent complex of law and political power gave rise to a new functional requirement—the legitimation of political authority. It is not a given that one person, or a handful of persons, can make decisions that are collectively binding on all.[3] They must be legitimated to do so. Only by establishing a convincing connection between law and political power with religious beliefs and practices could rulers be assured that the people followed their orders. While the legal system is stabilized by the sanctioning power of the state, political authority in turn depends on the legitimizing force of a law, which has a sacred origin. "Religion" owes its legitimizing force to the fact that it draws its power to convince from its own roots. It is rooted, *independently of politics,* in notions of salvation and calamity (*Heil und Unheil*) and in corresponding practices of coping with redemptive and menacing forces.[4]

Thus law and the monarch's judicial power owe their sacred aura to mythical narratives that connected ruling dynasties with the divine. At the same time, archaic ritual practices were transformed into state rituals—society as a whole represents itself in the figure of the ruler. And it is this symbolic dimension of the fusion of politics and religion for the description of which the concept of "the political" can properly be used. The collectivity sees itself mirrored in the ruler's self-representation as a political community that *intentionally*— i.e., consciously and deliberately—produces its social cohesion through the exercise of political power. Thus "the political" means the symbolic representation and collective self-understanding of a community that differs from tribal societies through a reflexive turn to a *conscious* rather than spontaneous form of social integration. In the self-understanding of this kind of polity the locus of control shifts toward collective action.[5] However, "the political" as such could not become a topic of discourse as long as mythic narratives remained the sole means of symbolic representation.

We owe the first discursively elaborated *conceptions of "the political"* to the nomos thinking (*Nomosdenken*) of Israel, China, and Greece and, more generally, to the cognitive advance of the Axial Age, that is, to the metaphysical and religious worldviews that were emerging at that time. These worldviews constructed perspectives that enabled the emerging intellectual elites made up of prophets, wise men, monks, and itinerant preachers to transcend events in the world, including political processes, and to adopt a detached stance toward them en bloc. From that time onward the political rulers were also open to criticism. The reference to a divinity outside the world or to the internal base of a cosmic law liberates the human mind from the grip of the narratively ordered flood of occurrences under the sway of mythical powers and makes an individual quest for salvation possible.

Once this transformation has taken place the political ruler can no longer be perceived as the manifestation of the divine but only as its human *representative*. From now on, he, as a human person, is also *subordinated* to the *nomos* in terms of which all human action must be measured. Because the axial worldviews make both legitimation and the critique of political authority possible at the same time, "the political" in the ancient empires was marked by an ambivalent tension between religious and political powers. Though the religiously backed belief in legitimacy can well be manipulated, it is never totally at the disposition of the ruler.[6] The precarious balance can be studied deep into the European Middle Ages in the relationship between the emperor and the pope. This bold historical jump hints at the extensive time span during which talk of "the political" had a clear meaning, namely, the symbolic order of the collective self-representation of political communities in the mirror image of rulers whose authority is legitimated by some sacred power.

Under the completely changed conditions of the modern period, Western conceptions of "the political," spelled out in Greek philosophy and Christian political theology, have lost their "setting in life" (*Sitz im Leben*), as it were. For Carl Schmitt, the unifying and integrating power of the political, as it had continued through the Holy Roman Empire, could survive only in the sovereign authority of Christian kings in the absolutist states of early modernity. In what follows I will first examine the thesis that "the political" assumed the shape of an absolutist regime à la Hobbes (2) and then briefly discuss the infamous conception through which Schmitt, from his perspective of an "era of statehood" drawing to a close, tried to renew the concept of the political under conditions of an authoritarian mass democracy (3).[7] Next I will use John Rawls's political liberalism as a counterexample (4) and finally explore whether we can still lend the religiously connotated concept of "the political" a rational meaning under the present conditions of a liberal democracy (5).

2. In the picture Carl Schmitt painted of the early modern state, political authority continues to draw its legitimation from belief in the authority of an all-powerful God; the rational features of the modern state apparatus even underline the conscious character of a form of social integration achieved by political intervention. From

this perspective, essential aspects of the traditional concept of "the political" once tailored to ancient empires now seem to be concentrated in the decision-making power of the modern sovereign. But, on closer historical inspection, this suggestive picture of continuity is misleading. In functional terms the formation of the early modern state can be understood as an answer to the explosive potential inherent in both the emerging capitalism and the confessional split. The modern state is tailored, on the one hand, to the economic imperatives of a system of economic exchange regulated by markets, hence operating independently from political structures, and, on the other, to the pacification of bloody religious wars.

Already at the beginning of the era, the new mode of production emerged as the driving force of a process of functional differentiation leading to a heterarchical reordering of society, while at the same time constraining the bureaucratic administration to the role of one social subsystem alongside others. This marked the gradual dissolution of mutual interpenetration of political and social structures, which had been typical of the old empires. The society that has become differentiated from the state has lost its "politomorphic" features. If we continue to understand "the political" as the symbolic medium of self-representation of a society that consciously influences the mechanisms of social integration, then the expansion of markets within territorial states involves, in fact, a certain degree of "depoliticization" of the society at large. But, contrary to Schmitt's diagnosis, a decisive step toward the neutralization of "the political" already occurred in *early* modernity within the framework of the sovereign state.

The citizens, having achieved economic independence, though at the cost of being forced into private domains, cannot be excluded indefinitely from civil rights and political participation. At the same time, the religious conflicts to which the Reformation gave rise, which could not be permanently suppressed through authoritarian toleration edicts from above, were, in the end, resolved through the recognition of religious freedom and free speech. During the early modern period these two developments already prefigured the "neutralization" of "the political," whereas Carl Schmitt wants to lay the blame for that kind of depoliticization at the door of the liberal regimes of the nineteenth and early twentieth centuries. In fact, the functional specification of the political administration already robs the early modern state of some of its power to permeate and structure society *as a whole*. Schmitt is mistaken in attributing the dissolution of the amalgamation of religion and politics that we associate with the political in its traditional form only to the time, when the constitutional revolutions of the late eighteenth century ratified the secularization of state authority.[8]

As to secularization, it is not only the challenge of the confessional split and the fact of pluralism that called for a secular state authority capable of treating the claims of all religious communities impartially; apart from that, democratic self-empowerment of citizens already strips the legitimation of political power of its metasocial character, in other words, of the reference to the warrant of a transcendent authority operating beyond society. This break with the traditional pattern of legitimation, in fact, raises the question of whether a justification of constitutional essentials in the secular terms of popular power and human rights closes off the dimension of "the political," thereby rendering the concept of "the political" with its religious connotations obsolete.[9] Or does the locus of "the political" merely shift from the level of the state to the democratic opinion- and will-formation of citizens within civil society? Against Carl Schmitt, we might ask: why shouldn't *the political* find an impersonal embodiment in the normative dimension of a democratic constitution? And what would this alternative mean for the relation between religion and politics in societies like ours?

In Carl Schmitt's view, liberalism is the force that robs politics of its significance for society as a whole—on the one hand, a functionally differentiated society is emancipated from the shaping force of politics and, on the other, the state is decoupled from a privatized religion that has lost its sting. Schmitt, therefore, develops a new and provocative concept of "the political" that is superficially adapted to mass democracy but preserves the authoritarian kernel of a sovereign power with its legitimizing relation to sacred history.

3. In liberalism Carl Schmitt combats the enemy that destroys "the political" through *neutralization*. What he means by that term is not only the withdrawal of politics into a functionally specified subsystem but also the loss of the religious aura of politics and the dissolution of sovereign decision-making power into democratic will formation. Liberalism "wants to dissolve metaphysical truth in a discussion."[10] Schmitt cherished clear sympathies for the political philosophy of counterrevolutionary thinkers such as de Maistre and de Bonald, but most of all for the militant thinker Donoso Cortes. This Spanish Catholic recognized that the era of Christian monarchy was over and, already in the mid nineteenth century, called for a "dictatorship of the sword" against the "deliberating class" of liberal citizens. Here the permanence of repression already reveals the intrinsically polemical nature of the political.

As a professor of constitutional and international law in the Weimar Republic, Carl Schmitt was, despite his own sympathies, well aware that the democratic idea of popular sovereignty was irrevocable. Yet for him two aspects of counterrevolutionary thought retained a more than merely nostalgic significance: the theological background of the "bloody decisive battle that has flared up today between Catholicism and atheist socialism" and,[11] on the other hand, the conviction that the "metaphysical kernel of the political" can only consist in the moment of "pure decision not based on reason and discussion and not justifying itself, that is . . . (in) an absolute decision created out of nothingness."[12]

In order to provide some kind of justification for such an existentialist concept of "the political," Schmitt constructs an identitarian conception of authoritarian mass democracy that is tailored to a homogeneous population and led by a charismatic leader.[13]

This *Fuehrer* is supposed to mobilize the nation against radical evil and weld its individual members together by exposing them to the fate of sacrifice and death. For Schmitt the struggle against the power of the "Antichrist" reaches across the whole eon between the "appearance of the Lord in the time of the Roman Caesar Augustus and the Lord's return at the end of time."[14] Since the fateful revolution of 1789, the camps in the struggle against the Antichrist are clearly divided by their partisanship for revelation and against enlightenment, for authority and against anarchism, for obedience to God and against human self-empowerment and progressivism.

Of course, Carl Schmitt's clericofascist conception of "the political" is a matter of the past, but it must serve as a warning to all those who want to revive political theology.[15] On the other hand, *the motivation* for such attempts continue to this day. John Rawls's political liberalism has not yet silenced the objections of a critical, postmetaphysical political theology,[16] even if today there prevails a more inconspicuous impulse to save *some* public religious foundation for democracy and the rule of law.[17] In one way or the other, the diagnosis of a progressive "negation of the political" does not seem to have been refuted. The remaining worry can be put in a nutshell: How can respect for the *inviolability* of human dignity, and, more generally, a public awareness of the relevance of normative questions, be kept alive in the face of growing and disarming systemic strains on the social integration of our political communities?[18]

4. In contrast to the classical works of the social contract tradition, which had stripped the concept of "the political" of any serious references to religion, John Rawls recognizes that the problem of the political impact of the role of religion in civil society has not been solved by the secularization of political authority per se. The secularization of the state is not the same as the secularization of society. This explains the air of paradox that to this day has fed a subliminal resentment within religious circles concerning the justification of constitutional principles "from reason alone."

Although a liberal constitution is designed in such a way as to guarantee all religious communities equal scope for freedom in civil society, it is, at the same time, supposed to shield the public bodies responsible for making collectively binding decisions from all religious influences. Those same people who are expressly authorized to practice their religion and to lead a pious life in their role as citizens are supposed to participate in a democratic process whose results must be kept free of any religious "contamination." Laicism pretends to resolve this paradox by privatizing religion entirely. But as long as religious communities play a vital role in civil society and the public sphere, deliberative politics is as much a product of the public use of reason on the part of *religious* citizens as on that of *nonreligious* citizens.

Certainly, the concept of "the political" remains a dubious heritage as long as political theology attempts to preserve metasocial connotations for whatever kind of state authority. In a liberal democracy, state power has lost its religious aura. And, in view of the fact of persisting pluralism, it is hard to see on which normative grounds the historical step toward the secularization of state power could ever be reversed. This in turn requires a justification of constitutional essentials and the outcomes of the democratic process in ways that are neutral toward the cognitive claims of competing worldviews. Democratic legitimacy is the only one available today. The idea of replacing it or complementing it by some presumably "deeper" grounding of the constitution in a generally binding way amounts to obscurantism. This is, however, not to deny the great insight of John Rawls: The liberal constitution itself must not ignore the contributions that religious groups can well make to the democratic process *within civil society*.

Therefore, even the collective identity of a liberal community cannot remain unaffected by the fact of the political interaction between religious and nonreligious parts of the population, provided they recognize each other as equal members of the same democratic community.[19] In this sense "the political," which has migrated from the level of the state to civil society, retains a reference to religion. It is not the conception of an overlapping consensus between competing doctrines and worldviews that is primarily relevant here. Rawls rather offers, with his idea of the "public use of reason," a promising key for explaining how the proper role of religion in the public sphere contributes to a rational interpretation of what we still might call "the political" as distinct from politics and policies.

The only element transcending administrative politics and institutionalized power politics emerges from the anarchic use of communicative freedoms that keeps alive the spring tide of informal flows of public communication from below. Through these channels alone, vital and nonfundamentalist religious communities can become a transformative force in the center of a democratic civil society—all the more so when frictions between religious and secular voices provoke inspiring controversies on normative issues and thereby stimulate an awareness of their relevance.

5. Rawls has sparked a lively discussion with his proposal for the rather restricted role of religion in the public sphere: "Reasonable comprehensive doctrines, religious or non-religious, may be introduced in public political discussion at any time, provided that in due course proper political reasons . . . are presented that are sufficient to support whatever the comprehensive doctrines introduced are said to support."[20] This Rawlsian "proviso" has been confronted with the empirical objection that many citizens *cannot* or *are not willing to* make the required separation between contributions expressed in religious terms and those expressed in secular language when they take political stances. Rawls furthermore faced the normative objection that a liberal constitution, which also exists to safeguard religious forms of life, must not inflict such an additional, and hence asymmetrical, burden on its religious citizens.[21] We can meet both objections with a different kind of implementing translation proviso.

According to this proposal, all citizens should be free to decide whether they want to use religious language in the public sphere. Were they to do so, they would, however, have to accept that the potential truth contents of religious utterances must be translated into a generally accessible language before they can find their way onto the agendas of parliaments, courts, or administrative bodies and influence their decisions. Instead of subjecting all citizens to the imposition of cleansing their public comments and opinions of religious rhetoric, an institutional filter should be established between informal communication in the public arena and formal deliberations of political bodies that yield to collectively binding decisions. This proposal achieves the liberal goal of ensuring that all legally enforceable and publicly sanctioned decisions can be formulated *and justified* in a universally accessible language without having to restrict the polyphonic diversity of public voices at its very source. To be sure, the "monolingual" contributions of religious citizens then depend on the translational efforts of cooperative fellow citizens if they are not to fall on deaf ears.

But such a regulation would no longer distribute burdens asymmetrically. Religious citizens who regard themselves as loyal members of a constitutional democracy must accept the translation proviso as the price to be paid for the neutrality of the state authority toward competing worldviews. For secular citizens, the same ethics of citizenship entails a complementary burden. By the duty of reciprocal accountability toward all citizens, including religious ones, they are obliged not to publicly dismiss religious contributions to political opinion and will formation as mere noise, or even nonsense, from the start.[22] Secular and religious citizens must meet in their public use of reason at eye level. For a democratic process the contributions of one side are no less important than those of the other side.

Thus a quite demanding epistemic mind-set that cannot be legally imposed is assumed on *both sides*.[23] Whether the expectations associated with the ethics of citizenship will, in fact, be fulfilled depends on complementary learning processes. From the religious side, the public use of reason demands a reflexive consciousness that

- relates itself to competing religions in a reasonable way,
- leaves decisions concerning mundane knowledge to the institutionalized sciences, and

- makes the egalitarian premises of the morality of human rights compatible with its own articles of faith.

On the other hand, the discursive confrontation with religious citizens endowed with equal rights demands from the secular side a similar reflection on the limits of a secular or postmetaphysical kind of reasoning. The insight that vibrant world religions may be bearers of "truth contents," in the sense of suppressed or untapped moral intuitions, is by no means a given for the secular portion of the population. A genealogical awareness of the religious origins of the morality of equal respect for everybody is helpful in this context. The occidental development has been shaped by the fact that philosophy continuously appropriates semantic contents from the Judeo-Christian tradition; and it is an open question whether this centuries-long learning process can be continued or even remains unfinished.

Admittedly, everything feared by Carl Schmitt in fact happened: the sovereign power of the king has been dissolved, disembodied, and dispersed in the communication flows of civil society, and it has at the same time assumed the shape of procedures, be it for general elections or the numerous deliberations and decisions of various political bodies. Claude Lefort is right in maintaining that sovereignty left behind an "empty place." But in the course of its democratic transformation, "the political" has not completely lost its association with religion.

In democratic discourse secular and religious citizens stand in a complementary relation. Both are involved in an interaction that is constitutive for a democratic process springing from the soil of civil society and developing through the informal communication networks of the public sphere. As long as religious communities remain a vital force in civil society, their contribution to the legitimation process reflects an at least indirect reference to religion, which "the political" retains even within a secular state. Although religion can neither be reduced to morality nor be assimilated to ethical value orientations, it nevertheless keeps alive an awareness of both elements. The public use of reason by religious and nonreligious citizens alike may well spur deliberative politics in a pluralist civil society and lead to the recovery of semantic potentials from religious traditions for the wider political culture.

Moreover, the eschatological impulse of a political theology revised in view of the democratic transformation of "the political" can also serve normative political theory as a reminder of the temporal dimension in which we raise normative claims.[24] In contrast to "ideal theories" of justice that draw the outlines of a just society beyond time and space, Johann Baptist Metz puts his finger on the difference between political justice in the Rawlsian sense and emancipatory justice in the biblical sense. He makes a case for the "sensitivity to time."[25] Only a dynamic understanding of any of our established liberal constitutions can sharpen our awareness of the fact that the democratic process is also a learning process, one often blocked by a deficient sense of what is lacking and what is still possible.[26] Any democratic constitution is and remains *a project*: Within the framework of the nation-state, it is oriented to the ever more thorough exhaustion of the normative substance of constitutional principles under changing historic conditions. And, at the global level, the universalistic meaning of human rights reminds us of the need to develop a constitutional frame for an emerging multicultural world society.

NOTES

1. Oliver Marchart, *Die politische Differenz* (Berlin: Suhrkamp, 2010); Thomas Bedorf and Kurt Röttgers, eds., *Das Politische und die Politik* (Berlin: Suhrkamp, 2010).

2. Claude Lefort, "The Permanence of the Theologico-Political," in Claude Lefort, *Democracy and Political Theory*, trans. David Macey (Cambridge: Polity, 1988), pp. 213–255, here p. 224.

3. On the conditions of the emergence of political power as a medium of social integration, see Jürgen Habermas, *Between Facts and Norms*, trans. W. Rehg (Cambridge: MIT Press, 1996), pp. 137–144.

4. Here I am using the term *religion* in the extended sense that includes myth and magic, cf. Martin Riesebrodt, *The Promise of Salvation: A Theory of Religion*, trans. S. Rendall (Chicago: University of Chicago Press, 2009).

5. Claude Lefort speaks in this context of *mise en forme* in the twofold sense of *mise en sens* and *mise en scène*: "We can say that the advent of a society capable of organizing social relations can come about only if it can institute the conditions of their intelligibility, and only if it can use a multiplicity of signs to arrive at a quasi-representation of itself." Lefort, "The Permanence of the Theologico-Political?" p. 219.

6. Riesebrodt, *The Promise of Salvation*, pp. 14, 17–18.

7. See the "Vorwort" to the new edition of Carl Schmitt, *Der Begriff des Politischen* (Berlin: Duncker und Humblot, 1963 [1932]), pp. 9–19.

8. I trace this distorted historical perception back to the fact that Carl Schmitt neglects the origins of modernity in medieval thought. See the recent account of Ludger Honnefelder, *Woher kommen wir? Ursprünge der Moderne im Denken des Mittelalters* (Berlin: Berlin University Press, 2008). Oddly enough, although Schmitt's own concept of God is basically shaped by nominalism, he devotes no attention to the long-term effects of the so-called nominalist revolution of the thirteenth century on the prevailing intellectual movements of the sixteenth and seventeenth centuries. On the following four points, see also Michael Allen Gillespie, *The Theological Origins of Modernity* (Chicago: University of Chicago Press, 2008):

- One path leads directly from the nominalist emphasis on divine omnipotence, from the contingency of human destinies at the mercy of God's unfathomable decrees, and from the constitutional weakness of a human understanding reliant upon empirical knowledge to the voluntarist conception of God and the Protestant doctrine of grace. By valorizing individual religious convictions, Protestantism taps into a spiritual source of individual autonomy that inspired both political indifference and resistance to the authority of the state.
- Another path leads from nominalism to modern science. By purging nature of divine ideas and advocating an ontology that attributes

existence only to individual entities, nominalism created preconditions for the emergence of empirical science in the present sense, which intensified the contrast between faith and knowledge and, in a pluralist society, promoted the public authority of mundane knowledge as a shared basis for universally accessible knowledge.

- More controversial is the influence of nominalism on Renaissance humanism, which fostered the anthropocentric turn in modern thought and the way in which the sciences contributed to the development of a rational alternative to the religious worldview.

- By contrast, the crucial influence of nominalism in undermining the foundations of Christian natural law is obvious. In addition, by striking a blow against the religious legitimation of power, it paved the way for those two discourses of the theory of knowledge and social contract theory that dominated seventeenth-century philosophy and provided a secular foundation for the legitimation of politics.

9. Thus Mark Lilla, *The Stillborn God: Religion, Politics, and the West* (New York: Knopf, 2007); for a critical response see Michael Kirwan, *Political Theology: An Introduction* (Darton, Longman and Hand, 2008).

10. Carl Schmitt, *Political Theology II: The Myth of the Closure of Any Political Theology*, trans. Michael Hoelzl and Graham Ward (Cambridge: Polity, 2008), p. 63.

11. Ibid., p. 59.

12. Ibid., p. 66. On Carl Schmitt's political theology see Heinrich Meier, *The Lesson of Carl Schmitt: Four Chapters on the Distinction Between Political Theology and Political Philosophy*, trans. M. Brainard (Chicago: University of Chicago Press, 1998).

13. For an inconspicuous introduction of such a voluntaristic concept of "the political," Schmitt takes as his starting point the concept of state sovereignty in international law. No matter how much a democratic constitution may strangle sovereignty in the domestic sphere, nothing prevents nation-states from affirming their sovereignty in external relations as long as the *ius ad bellumi* pemits them to conduct wars of aggression as they wish. Adopting this perspective of warring nations, Schmitt begins his 1927 work *Constitutional Theory* with a non-normative concept of the constitution: "The state does not *have* a constitution. . . . The state exists in a certain constitution, in other words, in an actually present

condition, occupying a *status* of unity and order." Carl Schmitt, *Constitutional Theory*, trans. and ed. J. Seitzer (Durham: Duke University Press, 2008, p.60 (translation amended). Schmitt does not understand the constituent power of "the nation" as a legally constituted unity of autonomous citizens, but rather as a concrete and organic collectivity. National membership is determined by common race, belief, common destiny, and tradition—in other words, by ascriptive features (ibid., p. 258). Accordingly, Schmitt shares a collectivistic and plebiscitary conception of democracy that is directed against the egalitarian conception of individual human rights and against a deliberative conception of politics: "Democratic equality is a *substantial* equality. Because all state citizens participate in this substantive component, they can be treated as equals, having an equal right to vote in general elections, etc." (ibid., p. 259; translation amended). But the people can exercise its right of participation only via acclamation; they can "express their consent or disapproval by . . . celebrating a leader or a suggestion . . . or denying the acclamation by silence or complaining" (ibid., p. 272). These theoretical moves are the result of a first problematic decision. Schmitt dissects the liberal constitution— against its express intention to link popular sovereignty and human rights—into "political" and "constitutional" components. This enables Schmitt to slip an identitarian conception of democracy as a "basis" underneath the constitutional superstructure. The law, he stipulates, places only loose fetters on politics anyway. Any state of emergency reveals that the "rule of law" is at the disposal of politics, that is, of an actual self-assertion of the nation. Ultimately the leader and the nation, in the person of its leader, must decide on who is friend or foe. The meaning of "the political" does not reside in the fight itself but in the ability of the political leaders "to distinguish between friend and foe" and the willingness of the nation to take up combat for the assertion of its own way of life.

This existentialist version continues to share essential features with the traditional concept of "the political." Certainly, the collective identity of the people is no longer defined in the legal terms of a sovereign state, but in the ethnonational concepts of political romanticism instead. However, the shared features of descent, tradition, and language cannot ensure the social cohesion of the collective by their supposed organic nature alone. Rather, the political leadership must continually mobilize the nation against external or internal enemies. This concept of "the political" assumed an even more authoritarian profile when it was accommodated, a few years after the publication of *Constitutional Theory*, to the Nazi movement.

14. Schmitt, *Political Theology II*, p. 86.

15. See the commentary on Schmitt in Jacob Taubes, ed., *Religionstheorie und Politische Theologie* (Munich: Wilhelm Fink, 1983).

16. Compare the impressive projects of a new political theology developed by Johann Baptist Metz and Jürgen Moltmann: Johann Baptist Metz, *Faith in History and Society* (London: Burns and Oates, 1980); Jürgen Moltmann, *Theology of Hope* (London: SCM, 1967).

17. Charles Taylor, "Die Bedeutung des Säkularismus," in Rainer Forst, Martin Hartmann, Martin Saar, and Rahel Jaeggi, eds., *Sozialphilosophie und Kritik* (Frankfurt: Suhrkamp, 2009), pp. 672–696.

18. Lutz Wingert, "Was ist und was heißt 'unverfügbar'?" in Forst et al., *Sozialphilosophie und Kritik*, pp. 384–408.

19. See Taylor's phenomenologically convincing analysis in Charles Taylor, *A Secular Age* (Cambridge: Harvard University Press, 2007), especially chapter 15, pp. 539ff.

20. Rawls, "The Idea of Public Reason Revisited," *University of Chicago Law Review* 64 (Summer 1997): 765–807, citation at 783.

21. For a résumé of these objections, see Jürgen Habermas, "Religion in the Public Sphere," in Jürgen Habermas, *Between Naturalism and Religion*, trans. Ciaran Cronin (Cambridge: Polity, 2008), pp. 114–147.

22. For an opposing view, see Cristina Lafont, "Religion in the Public Sphere," *Philosophy and Social Criticism* 35 (2009): 127–150: "The corollary of allowing citizens of faith to use exclusively religious reasons for political advocacy in the informal public sphere is that secular citizens must exercise constraint concerning their 'secularist attitudes.' . . . In contradistinction to religious citizens, they should not make public use of their sincere beliefs, if these beliefs happen to be of a secularist type that contradict the possible truth of religious claims" (135). Quite apart from the fact that the "truth" of religious validity claims is not in question here, but rather the potentially translatable *truth content* of religious utterances, the exclusion of secularism from the public use of reason is, in fact, an implication of the ethics of citizenship that is accepted by citizens who are loyal to the constitution. A *public practice* of secularism would amount to secular citizens not taking their fellow citizens seriously as modern contemporaries because of their religious outlook. However, this stance would be no

more compatible with a reciprocity of recognition than it would be with a mutual perspective taking in discursive exchanges. The objection that the proposed expectation could tempt secular citizens into insincerity has no force for a discourse-theoretical understanding of the democratic process. Apart from the fact that motives for actual voting behavior are not, in any case, subject to any form of regulation, only public utterances, hence actual contributions to the formation of opinions and consensus building, and not mind-sets, are relevant for the legitimizing power of democratic discourses. See Jürgen Habermas, "Die Dialektik der Säkularisierung," *Blätter für deutsche und internationale Politik* 4 (2008): 33–46.

23. That is the point of my argument in Habermas, "Religion in the Public Sphere," pp. 135–147.

24. Thomas Polednitschek, Michael J. Rainer, and José A. Zamora, eds., *Theologisch-politische Vergewisserungen* (Münster: Lit, 2009).

25. Johann Baptist Metz, *Memoria Passionis* (Freiburg: Herder, 2006).

26. Chistrian F. Rostboell, "Emancipation or Accommodation," *Philosophy and Social Criticism* 34, no. 7 (2008): 707–736.

WHY WE NEED A RADICAL REDEFINITION OF SECULARISM

CHARLES TAYLOR

I

It is generally agreed that modern democracies have to be "secular." There is perhaps a problem, a certain ethnocentricity, involved in this term. But even in the Western context the term is not limpid. What in fact does it mean? I believe that there are at least two models of what constitutes a secular regime.

Both involve some kind of separation of church and state. The state can't be officially linked to some religious confession; except in a vestigial and largely symbolic sense, as in England or Scandinavia. But secularism requires more than this. The pluralism of society requires that there be some kind of neutrality, or "principled distance," to use Rajeev Bhargava's term.[1]

If we try to examine it further secularism involves in fact a complex requirement. There is more than one good sought here. We can single out three, which we can class in the three categories of the French Revolutionary trinity: liberty, equality, fraternity. 1. No one must be forced in the domain of religion or basic belief. This is what is often defined as religious liberty, including of course, the freedom not to believe. This is what is also described as the "free exercise" of religion, in the terms of the U.S. First Amendment. 2. There must be equality between people of different faiths or basic belief; no religious outlook or (religious or areligious) Weltanschauung can enjoy a privileged status, let alone be adopted as the official view of the state. Then 3. all spiritual families must be heard, included in the ongoing process of determining what the society is about (its political identity), and how it is going to realize these goals (the exact regime of rights and privileges). This (stretching the point a little) is what corresponds to "fraternity."

These goals can, of course, conflict; sometimes we have to balance the goods involved here. Moreover, I believe that we might add a fourth goal: that we try as much as possible to maintain relations of harmony and comity between the supporters of different religions and Weltanschauungen (maybe this is what really deserves to be called "fraternity," but I am still attached to the neatness of this schema, with only the three traditional goods.)

Sometimes the claim seems to be made, on behalf of one or other definition of secularism, that it can resolve the question of how to realize these goals in the domain of timeless principle and that no further input, or negotiation is required to define them for our society now. The basis for these principles can be found in reason alone or in some outlook that is itself free from religion, purely *laïque*. Jacobins are on this wavelength, as was the first Rawls.

The problem with this is that a. there is no such set of timeless principles that can be determined, at least in the detail they must be for a given political system, by pure reason alone; and b. situations differ very much, and require different kinds of concrete realization of agreed general principles, so that some degree of working out is necessary in each situation. It follows that c. dictating the principles from some supposedly higher authority above the fray violates 3. It deprives certain spiritual families of a voice in this working out. And therefore d. this leaves us very often with difficult conflicts and dilemmas between our basic goals.

We have a good illustration of b in the way that the issues concerning secularism have evolved in different Western societies in recent decades, because the faiths represented in those societies have changed. We need to alter the way in which we proceed when the range of religions or basic philosophies expands: e.g., contemporary Europe or America with the arrival of substantive communities of Muslims.

In relation to c, we have the recent legislation in France against wearing the hijab in schools. Normally, this kind of thing needs to be negotiated. The host country is often forced to send a double message: i. you can't do that here (kill blaspheming authors, practice FGM) and ii. we invite you to be part of our consensus-building process. These tend to run against each other; i hinders and renders ii less plausible. All the more reason to avoid where possible the unilateral application of i. Of course, sometimes it is not possible. Certain basic laws have to be observed. But the general principle is that religious groups must be seen as much as interlocutors and as little as menace as the situation allows.

These groups also evolve if they're in a process of redefinition of this kind in a democratic, liberal context. José Casanova has pointed out how American Catholicism was originally targeted in the nineteenth century as inassimilable to democratic mores, in ways very analogous to the suspicions that nag people over Islam today. The subsequent history has shown how American Catholicism evolved and, in the process, changed world Catholicism in significant ways. There is no reason written into the essence of things why a similar evolution cannot take place in Muslim communities.[2] If this doesn't happen, it will in all likelihood be because of prejudice and bad management.

Now I believe that one of our basic difficulties in dealing with these problems is that we have the wrong model, which has a continuing hold on our minds. We think that secularism (or *laïcité*) has to do with the relation of the state and religion; whereas in fact it has to do with the (correct) response of the democratic state to diversity. If we look at the three goals, they have in common that they are concerned with 1. protecting people in their belonging to and/or practice of whatever outlook they choose or find themselves in; with 2. treating people equally whatever their choice; and 3. giving them all a hearing. There is no reason to single out religion, as against nonreligious, "secular" (in another widely used sense), or atheist viewpoints.

Indeed, the point of state neutrality is precisely to avoid favoring or disfavoring not just religious positions but any basic position, religious or nonreligious. We can't favor Christianity over Islam, but also religion over against nonbelief in religion or vice versa.

One of the ways of demonstrating the superiority of the three-principle model of secularism, over that which is fixated on religion, is that it would never allow one to misrecognize the regime founded by Atatürk as genuinely secular, making light as it does of the fundamental principles and even of the separation of state and religious institutions.

This also shows the value of the late-Rawlsian formulation for a secular state. This cleaves very strongly to certain political principles: human rights, equality, the rule of law, democracy. These are the very bases of the state, which must support them. But this political ethic can be and is shared by people of very different basic outlooks (what Rawls calls "comprehensive views of the good"). A Kantian will justify the rights to life and freedom by pointing to the dignity of rational agency; a utilitarian will speak of the necessity to treat beings who can experience joy and suffering in such a way as to maximize the first and minimize the second. A Christian will speak of humans as made in the image of God. They concur on the principles, but differ on the deeper reasons for holding to this ethic. The state must uphold the ethic, but must refrain from favoring any of the deeper reasons.

2

The idea that secularism makes a special case of religion arises from the history of its coming to be in the West (as does, indeed, the name). To put it briefly, there are two important founding contexts for this kind of regime, the U.S. and France. In the U.S. case, the whole range of comprehensive views, or deeper reasons, were in the original case variants of (Protestant) Christianity, stretching to a smattering of Deists. Subsequent history has widened the palette of views beyond Christianity and then beyond religion. But, in the original case, the positions between which the state must be neutral were all religious. Hence the First Amendment: Congress shall pass no law establishing religion or impeding the free exercise thereof.

The word *secularism* didn't appear in the early decades of American public life. But this is a sign that a basic problem had not yet been faced. Because the First Amendment concerned the separation of church and state, it opened the possibility of giving a place to *religion* that no one would accept today. Thus, in the 1830s, a judge of the Supreme Court could argue that while the First Amendment forbade the identification of the federal government with any church, since all the churches were Christian (and in effect Protestant), one could invoke the principles of Christianity in interpreting the law.

For Judge Joseph Story, the goal of the first amendment was "to exclude all rivalry among Christian sects," but nevertheless "Christianity ought to receive encouragement from the state." Christianity was essential to the state because the belief in "a future state of rewards and punishments" is "indispensable to the administration of justice." What is more, "it is impossible for those who believe in the truth of Christianity, as a divine revelation, to doubt, that it is a special duty of government to foster, and encourage it among the citizens."[3]

This primacy of Christianity was upheld even later in the nineteenth century. As late as 1890, thirty-seven of the forty-two existing states recognized the authority of God in the preambles or in the text of their constitutions. A unanimous judgment of the Supreme Court of 1892 declared that if one wanted to describe "American life as expressed by its laws, its business, its customs and its society, we find everywhere a clear recognition of the same truth . . . that this is a Christian nation."[4]

In the latter part of the century, resistance began to build to this conception, but a National Reform Association was founded in 1863 with the following goal:

> The object of this Society shall be to maintain existing Christian features in the American government . . . to secure such an amendment to the Constitution of the United States as will declare the nation's allegiance to Jesus Christ and its acceptance of the moral laws of the Christian religion, and so as to indicate that this is a Christian nation, and place all the Christian laws, institutions, and usages of our government on an undeniable legal basis in the fundamental law of the land.

After 1870, the battle was joined by the supporters of this narrow view, on one hand, and those who wanted a real opening to all other religions and also to nonreligion, on the other. These included not only Jews but also Catholics who (rightly) saw the "Christianity" of the NRA as excluding them. It was in this battle that the word *secular* first appears on the American scene as a key term, and very often in its polemical sense of non- or antireligious.[5]

In the French case, laïcité came about in a struggle *against* a powerful church. The strong temptation was for the state itself to stand on a moral basis independent from religion. Marcel Gauchet shows how Renouvier laid the grounds for the outlook of the Third Republic radicals in their battle against the church. The state has to be "moral et enseignant" (moral and a teaching agency). It has "charge d'âmes aussi bien que toute Église ou communauté, mais à titre plus universel" (charge of souls just as does the church or religious community, but on a more universal scale). Morality is the key criterion. In order not to be under the church, the state must have "une morale indépendante de toute religion" (a morality independent of all religion), and enjoy a "suprématie morale" (moral supremacy) in relation to all religions. The basis of this morality is liberty. In order to hold its own before religion, the morality underlying the state has to be based on more than just utility or feeling; it needs a real "théologie rationnelle," like that of Kant.[6] The wisdom of Jules Ferry, and later of Aristide Briand and Jean Juarès, saved France at the time of the Separation (1905) from such a lop-sided regime, but the notion stuck that laïcité was all about controlling and managing religion.

If we move, however, beyond such originating contexts, and look at the kinds of societies in which we are now living in the West, the first feature that strikes us is the wide diversity not only of religious views but also of those that involve no religion, not to speak of those that are unclassifiable in this dichotomy. Reasons 1, 2, and 3 require that we treat evenhandedly all of these.

3

This fixation on religion is complex, and it is bound up with two other features we often find in the debates on secularism: the first is the tendency to define secularism or laïcité in terms of some institutional arrangement, rather than starting from the goals that I propose. And so you hear mantra-type formulae like "the separation of church and state" or the necessity of removing religion from public space ("les espaces de la République," as in the recent French debate). The second follows from the first, or may easily seem to. If the whole matter is defined by one institutional formula, then one must just determine which arrangement of things best meets this formula, and there is no need to think further. One cannot find oneself in a dilemma, as will easily happen if one is pursuing more than one goal, because here there is just one master formula.

Hence one often hears these mantras employed as argument stoppers, the ultimate decisive response that annuls all objections. In the U.S., people invoke the "Wall of Separation" as the ultimate criterion, and hyper-Republicans in France cite laïcité as the final word.

(Of course, if one consulted the First Amendment of the U.S. Constitution one would find two goals mentioned, the rejection of establishment and the assurance of "free exercise." It is not inconceivable that these could conflict.)

This kind of move amounts, from the standpoint I'm adopting here, to a fetishization of the favored institutional arrangements. Whereas one should start from the goals and derive the concrete arrangements from these. It is not that some separation of church and state, some mutual autonomy of governing and religious institutions, will not be an inescapable feature of any secularist regime. And the same goes for the neutrality of the public institutions. These are both indispensable. But what these requirements mean in practice ought to be determined by how we can maximize our three (or four) basic goals.

Take, for example, the wearing of the hijab by Muslim women in public schools, which has been a hot issue in a number of Western democracies. In France, pupils in public schools were famously forbidden the headscarf, seen as a "signe religieux ostantatoire" (ostentatious religious sign), according to the notorious Loi Stasi of 2004. In certain German Laender, pupils can wear it, but not teachers. In the UK and other countries, there is no general interdict, but the individual schools can decide.

What are the reasons for this variation? Plainly, in all these cases, legislators and administrators were trying to balance two goals. One was the maintenance of neutrality in public institutions seen (rightly) as an essential entailment of goal 2: equality between all basic beliefs. The other was goal 1, ensuring the maximum possible religious liberty or, in its most general form, liberty of conscience. Goal 1 seems to push us toward permitting the hijab anywhere. But various arguments were made to override this in the French and German cases. For the Germans, what was disturbing was that someone in authority in a public institution should be religiously marked, as it were. In the French case, an attempt was made to cast doubt on the proposition that wearing the hijab was a free act. There were dark suggestions that the girls were being forced by their families or by their male peers to adopt this dress code. This was one argument, frequently used, however dubious it might appear in the light of the sociological research carried out among the pupils themselves, that the Stasi Commission largely ignored.

The other main argument was that wearing of the headscarf in school was less an act of piety than a statement of hostility against the republic and its essential institution of laïcité. This was the meaning behind the introduction of the concept of "signe ostantatoire." A smaller, more discrete sign would be no problem, argued the Stasi Commission, but these attention-grabbing features of dress were meant to make a highly controversial statement. It was in vain that Muslim women protested that "le foulard n'est pas un signe" (the headscarf is not a sign).

So, on one level, we can see that these different national answers to the same question reflect different takes on how to balance the two main goals of a secular regime. But on another level, the dilemma and its resolution remain hidden under the illusion that there is only one principle here, say, laïcité and its corollary of the neutrality of public institutions or spaces ("les espaces de la République"). It's just a matter of applying an essential feature of our republican regime; there is no need or place for choice or the weighing of different aims.

Perhaps the most pernicious feature of this fetishization is that it tends to hide from view the real dilemmas we encounter in this realm that leap into view once we recognize the plurality of principles at stake.

4

We should be aware that this fetishization reflects a deep feature of life in modern democracies. We can see why as soon as we ponder what is involved in self-government, what is implied in the basic mode of legitimation of states, that they are founded on popular sovereignty. For the people to be sovereign, it needs to form an entity and have a personality.

The revolutions that ushered in regimes of popular sovereignty transferred the ruling power from a king onto a *nation* or a *people*. In the process, they invent a new kind of collective agency. These terms existed before, but the thing they now indicate, this new kind of agency, was something unprecedented, at least in the immediate context of early modern Europe. Thus the notion "people" could certainly be applied to the ensemble of subjects of the kingdom, or to the nonelite strata of society, but before the turnover it hadn't indicated an entity that could decide and act together, to which one could attribute a *will*.

But for people to act together, in other words, to deliberate in order to form a common will on which they will act, requires a high degree of common commitment, a sense of common identification. A society of this kind presupposes trust, the basic trust that members and constituent groups have to have, the confidence that they are really part of the process, that they will be listened to and their views taken account of by the others. Without this mutual commitment, this trust will be fatally eroded.

And so we have in the modern age a new kind of collective agency. It is one with which its members identify, typically as the realization/bulwark of their freedom and/or the locus of their national/cultural expression (or most often, some combination of the two). Of course, in premodern societies, too, people often "identified" with the regime, with sacred kings or hierarchical orders. They were often willing subjects. But in the democratic age we identify as free agents. That is why the notion of "popular will" plays a crucial role in the legitimating idea.[7]

This means that the modern democratic state has generally accepted common purposes, or reference points, the features whereby it can lay claim to being the bulwark of freedom and locus of expression of its citizens. Whether or not these claims are actually founded, the state must be so imagined by its citizens if it is to be legitimate.

So a question can arise for the modern state for which there is no analogue in most premodern forms: What, or whom, is this state for? Whose freedom? Whose expression? The question seems to make no sense applied to, say, the Austrian or Turkish Empires—unless one answered the "whom for?" question by referring to the Habsburg or Ottoman dynasties, and this would hardly give you their legitimating ideas.

This is the sense in which a modern state has what I want to call a political identity, defined as the generally accepted answer to the "what/whom for?" question. This is distinct from the identities of its members, namely, the reference points, many and varied, that, for each of these, defines what is important in their lives. There better be some overlap, of course, if these members are to feel strongly identified with the state; but the identities of individuals and constituent groups will generally be richer and more complex as well as being often quite different from each other.[8]

In other words, a modern democratic state demands a "people" with a strong collective identity. Democracy obliges us to show much more solidarity and much more commitment to one another in our joint political project than was demanded by the hierarchical and authoritarian societies of yesteryear. In the good old days of the Austro-Hungarian Empire, the Polish peasant in Galicia could be altogether oblivious of the Hungarian country squire, the bourgeois of Prague, or the Viennese worker without this in the slightest threatening the stability of the state. On the contrary. This condition of things only becomes untenable when ideas about popular government start to circulate. This is the moment when subgroups, which will not, or cannot, be bound together, start to demand their own states. This is the era of nationalism, of the breakup of empires.

I have been discussing the political necessity of a strong common identity for modern democratic states in terms of the requirement of forming a people, a deliberative unit. But this is also evident in a number of other ways. Thinkers in the civic humanist tradition, from Aristotle through to Arendt, have noted that free societies require a higher level of commitment and participation than despotic or authoritarian ones. Citizens have to do for themselves, as it were, what otherwise the rulers would do for them. But this will only happen if these citizens feel a strong bond of identification with their political community and hence with those who share with them in this.

From another angle, again, because these societies require strong commitment to do the common work, and because a situation in which some carried the burdens of participation and others just enjoyed the benefits would be intolerable, free societies require a high level of mutual trust. In other words, they are extremely vulnerable to mistrust on the part of some citizens in relation to others, that the latter are not really assuming their commitments—e.g., that others are not paying their taxes or are cheating on welfare or, as employers, are benefiting from a good labor market without assuming any of the social costs. This kind of mistrust creates extreme tension and threatens to unravel the whole skein of the mores of commitment that democratic societies need to operate. A continuing and constantly renewed mutual commitment is an essential basis for taking the measures needed to renew this trust.

The relation between nation and state is often considered from a unilateral point of view, as if it were always the nation that sought to provide itself with a state. But there is also the opposite process. In order to remain viable, states sometimes seek to create a feeling of common belonging. This is an important theme in the history of Canada, for example. To form a state, in the democratic era, a society is forced to undertake the difficult and never-to-be-completed task of defining its collective identity.

Thus what I have been calling political identity is extremely important in modern democratic states. And this identity is usually defined partly in terms of certain basic principles (democracy, human rights, equality), and partly in terms of their historic, or linguistic, or religious traditions. It is understandable that features of this identity can take on a quasi-sacred status, for to alter or undermine them can seem to threaten the very basis of unity without which a democratic state cannot function.

It is in this context that certain historical institutional arrangements can appear to be untouchable. They may appear as an essential part of the basic principles of the regime, but they will also come to be seen as a key component of its historic identity. This is what one sees with laïcité as invoked by many French *républicains*. The irony is that, in the face of a modern politics of (multicultural) identity, they invoke this principle as a crucial feature of (French) identity. This is unfortunate but very understandable. It is one illustration of a general truth: that contemporary democracies, as they progressively diversify, will have to undergo redefinitions of their historical identities, which may be far-reaching and painful.

5

At this juncture I would like to discuss an interesting point that Habermas reminds us of in his paper "The Political": originally political authority was defined and justified in cosmic-religious terms. It was defined within the terms of a "political theology."[9] But Habermas seems to think that modern secular states might do altogether without some analogous concept, and this seems to me not quite right.

The crucial move that we see in the modern West from the seventeenth century, the move that takes us out of the cosmic religious conceptions of order, establishes a new "bottom-up" view of society, as existing for the protection and mutual benefit of its (equal) members. There is a strong normative view attached to this new conception, which I've called the "modern moral order."[10] It enshrines basically three principles (on one possible enumeration): 1. the rights and liberties of the members, 2. the equality among them (which has of course been variously interpreted and has mutated toward more radical conceptions over time), and 3. the principle that rule is based on consent (which has also been defended in more and less radical forms).

These basic norms have been worked out in a host of different philosophical anthropologies and according to very different concepts of human sociability. It very soon transcended the atomism that narrowed the vision of its early formulators, like Locke and Hobbes. But the basic norms remain and are more or less inseparable from modern liberal democracies.

The rejection of cosmic-religious embedding thus was accomplished by a new conception of "the political," a new basic norm, which as Lefort suggests involved its own representation of political authority, but one in which the central spot remains paradoxically empty. If the notion of sovereignty is retained, no one person or group can be identified with it.

Democratic societies are organized not necessarily around a "civil religion," as Rousseau claimed, but certainly around a strong "philosophy of civility," enshrining the three norms, which in contemporary societies are often expressed as 1. human rights, 2. equality and nondiscrimination, and 3. democracy.

But, in certain cases, there can be a civil religion: a religious view incorporating and justifying the philosophy of civility. This was arguably so for the young American republic. It was adopting a form that was clearly part of God's providential plan for mankind ("We hold these truths to be self-evident, that men were *created* equal . . . "). Or it can alternatively be part of a non- or even antireligious ideology, as with the First French Republic. One can even argue that all-englobing views of this kind seem more "natural" to many of our contemporaries. After all, the principles of our civil philosophy seem to call for deeper grounding. If it's very important that we agree on the principles, then surely things are much more stable if we also accept a common grounding. Or, so it may appear, and the centuries-long tradition of political life seems to testify for this idea.

For, indeed, the overlapping consensus between different founding views on a common philosophy of civility is something quite new in history and relatively untried. It is consequently hazardous. And, besides, we often suspect that those with different basic views can't really subscribe to these principles, not the way we do! (Because, as "we" know, "atheists can't have principles," or, as [another] "we" knows, "religions are all against liberty and /or equality.")

The problem is that a really diverse democracy can't revert to a civil religion, or antireligion, however comforting this might be, without betraying its own principles. We are condemned to live an overlapping consensus.

6

We have seen how this strongly motivated move to fetishize our historical arrangements can prevent our seeing our secular regime in a more fruitful light, which foregrounds the basic goals we are seeking and allows us to recognize and reason about the dilemmas which we face. But this connects to the other main cause of confusion I have already cited, our fixation on religion as the problem. In fact, we have moved in many Western countries from an original phase, in which secularism was a hard-won achievement warding off some form of religious domination, to a phase of such widespread diversity of basic beliefs, religious and areligious, that only clear focus on the need to balance freedom of conscience and equality of respect can allow us to take the measure of the situation. Otherwise we risk needlessly limiting the religious freedom of immigrant minorities, on the strength of our historic institutional arrangements, while sending a message to these same minorities that they by no means enjoy equal status with the long-established mainstream.

Think of the argument of the German Laender that forbade the headscarf for teachers. These are authority figures, surely; but is our idea that only unmarked people can be authority figures? That those whose religious practices make them stand out in this context don't belong in positions of authority in this society? This is maybe the wrong message to inculcate in children in a rapidly diversifying society.

But the fixation on religion as the problem is not just a historical relic. Much of our thought, and some of our major thinkers, remain stuck in the old rut. They want to make a special thing of religion, but not always for very flattering reasons.

What are we to think of the idea, entertained by Rawls for a time, that one can legitimately ask of a religiously and philosophically diverse democracy that everyone deliberate in a language of reason alone, leaving their religious views in the vestibule of the public sphere? The tyrannical nature of this demand was rapidly appreciated by Rawls, to his credit. But we ought to ask why the proposition arose in the first place. Rawls's point in suggesting this restriction was that everyone should use a language with which they could reasonably expect their fellow citizens to agree. The idea seems to be something like this. Secular reason is a language that everyone speaks and can argue and be convinced in. Religious languages operate outside this discourse by introducing extraneous premises that only believers can accept. So let's all talk the common language.

What underpins this notion is something like an epistemic distinction. There is secular reason, which everyone can use and reach conclusions by, conclusions, that is, with which everyone can agree. Then there are special languages, which introduce extra assumptions that might even contradict those of ordinary secular reason. These are much more epistemically fragile; in fact, you won't be convinced by them unless you already hold them. So religious reason either comes to the same conclusions as secular reason, but then it is superfluous, or it comes to contrary conclusions, and then it is dangerous and disruptive. This is why it needs to be sidelined.

As for Habermas, he has always marked an epistemic break between secular reason and religious thought, with the advantage on the side of the first. Secular reason suffices to arrive at the normative conclusions we need, such as establishing the legitimacy of the democratic state and defining our political ethic. Recently, his position on religious discourse has considerably evolved; to the point of recognizing that its "potential [to articulate more intuitions] makes religious speech into a serious vehicle for possible truth contents." But the basic epistemic distinction still holds for him. Thus, when it comes to the official language of the state, religious references have to be expunged. "In parliament, for example, the rules of procedure must empower the house leader to strike religious positions or justifications from the official transcript."[11]

Do these positions of Rawls and Habermas show that they have not yet understood the normative basis for the contemporary secular state? I believe that they are on to something, in that there are zones of a secular state in which the language used has to be neutral. But these do not include citizen deliberation, as Rawls at first thought, or even deliberation in the legislature, as Habermas seems to think from the aforementioned quote. This zone can be described as the official language of the state: the language in which legislation, administrative decrees, and court judgments must be couched. It is self-evident that a law before Parliament couldn't contain a justifying clause of the type: "Whereas the Bible tells us that . . . " And the same goes, mutatis mutandis, for the justification of a judicial decision in the court's verdict. But this has nothing to do with the specific nature of religious language. It would be equally improper to have a legislative clause: "Whereas Marx has shown that religion is the opium of the people" or "Whereas Kant has shown that the only thing good without qualification is a good will." The grounds for both these kinds of exclusions is the neutrality of the state.

The state can be neither Christian nor Muslim nor Jewish, but, by the same token, it should also be neither Marxist, nor Kantian, nor utilitarian. Of course, the democratic state will end up voting laws that (in the best case) reflect the actual convictions of its citizens, which will be either Christian or Muslim, etc, through the whole gamut of views held in a modern society. But the decisions can't be framed in a way that gives special recognition to one of these views. This is not easy to do; the lines are hard to draw, and they must always be drawn anew. But such is the nature of the enterprise that is the modern secular state. And what better alternative is there for diverse democracies?[12]

Now the notion that state neutrality is basically a response to diversity has trouble making headway among "secular" people in the West, who remain oddly fixated on religion as something strange and perhaps even threatening. This stance is fed by all the conflicts, past and present, of liberal states with religion, but also by a specifically epistemic distinction: religiously informed thought is somehow less *rational* than purely "secular" reasoning. The attitude has a political ground (religion as threat), but also an epistemological one (religion as a faulty mode of reason).[13]

I believe we can see these two motifs in a popular contemporary book, Mark Lilla's *The Stillborn God*. On one hand, Lilla wants to claim that there is a great gulf between thinking informed by political theology and "thinking and talking about politics exclusively in human terms."[14] Moderns have effected "the liberation, isolation, and clarification of distinctively political questions, apart from speculations about the divine nexus. Politics became, intellectually speaking, its own realm deserving independent investigation and serving the limited aim of providing the peace and plenty necessary for human dignity. That was the Great Separation."[15] Such metaphors of radical separation imply that human-centred political thought is a more reliable guide to answer the questions in its domain than theories informed by political theology.

So much for the epistemological ranking. But then, toward the end of his book, Lilla calls on us not to lose our nerve and allow the Great Separation to be reversed,[16] which seems to imply that there are dangers in doing so. The return of religion in this sense would be full of menace.[17]

7

This phenomenon deserves fuller examination. Ideally, we should look carefully at the double grounds for this stance of distrust, comment on these, and then say something about the possible negative political consequences of maintaining this stance. But in this chapter I shall only really have space to look at the roots of the epistemological ground.

I think this has its source in what one might call a myth of the Enlightenment. There certainly is a common view that sees the Enlightenment (*Aufklärung*, *Lumières*) as a passage from darkness to light, that is, as an absolute, unmitigated move from a realm of thought full of error and illusion to one where the truth is at last available. To this one must immediately add that a counterview defines "reactionary" thought: the Enlightenment would be an unqualified move into error, a massive forgetting of salutary and necessary truths about the human condition.

In the polemics around modernity, more nuanced understandings tend to get driven to the wall, and these two slug it out. Arnold's phrase about "ignorant armies clashing by night" comes irresistibly to mind.

But what I want to do here, rather than bemoaning this fact, is to try to explain what underlies the understanding of Enlightenment as an absolute, unmitigated step forward. This is what I see as the "myth" of the Enlightenment. (One can't resist this jab, because "myth" is often cited as what Enlightenment has saved us from.)

This is worth doing, I believe, because the myth is more widespread than one might think. Even sophisticated thinkers, who might repudiate it when it is presented as a general proposition, seem to be leaning on it in other contexts.

Thus there is a version of what Enlightenment represents that sees it as our stepping out of a realm in which Revelation, or religion in general, counted as a source of insight about human affairs into a realm in which these are now understood in purely this-worldly or human terms. Of course, that some people have made this passage is not what is in dispute. What is questionable is the idea that this move involves the self-evident epistemic gain of our setting aside consideration of dubious truth and relevance and concentrating on matters we can settle that are obviously relevant. This is often represented as a move from Revelation to reason alone (Kant's *blosse Vernunft*).

Clearer examples are found in contemporary political thinkers, for instance, Rawls and Habermas. For all their differences, they seem to reserve a special status for nonreligiously informed Reason (let's call this "reason alone"), as though a. the latter were able to resolve certain moral-political issues in a way that can legitimately satisfy any honest, unconfused thinker and b. where religiously based conclusions will always be dubious and in the end only convincing to people who have already accepted the dogmas in question.

This surely is what lies behind the idea I mentioned earlier in section 6, entertained for a time in different form by both thinkers, that one can restrict the use of religious language in the sphere of public reason. We must mention again that this proposition has been largely dropped by both; but we can see that the proposition itself makes no sense, unless something like a + b is true. Rawls's point in suggesting this restriction was that public reason must be couched in terms that could in principle be universally agreed upon. The notion was that the only terms meeting this standard were those of reason alone (a), while religious language by its very nature would fail to do so (b).

Before proceeding farther, I should just say that this distinction in rational credibility between religious and nonreligious discourse, supposed by a + b, seems to me utterly without foundation. It may turn out at the end of the day that religion is founded on an illusion, and hence that what is derived from it less credible. But, until we actually reach that place, there is no a priori reason for greater suspicion being directed at it. The credibility of this distinction depends on the view that some quite "this-worldly" argument *suffices* to establish certain moral-political conclusions. I mean "satisfy" in the sense of a: it should legitimately be convincing to any honest, unconfused thinker. There are propositions of this kind, ranging from "$2+2=4$" all the way to some of the better-founded deliverances of modern natural science. But the key beliefs we need, for instance, to establish our basic political morality are not among them. The two most widespread this-worldly philosophies in our contemporary world, utilitarianism and Kantianism, in their different versions, all have points at which they fail to convince honest and unconfused people. If we take key statements of our contemporary political morality, such as those attributing rights to human beings as such, say the right to life, I cannot see how the fact that we are desiring/enjoying/suffering beings, or the perception that we are rational agents, should be any surer basis for this right than the fact that we are made in the image of God. Of course, our being capable of suffering is one of those basic unchallengeable propositions, in the sense of a, as our being creatures of God is not, but what is less sure is what follows normatively from the first claim.

Of course, this distinction would be much more credible if one had a "secular" argument for rights that was watertight. And this probably accounts for the difference between me and Habermas on this score. He finds this secure foundation in a "discourse ethic," which I unfortunately find quite unconvincing.

The a + b distinction, applied to the moral-political domain, is one of the fruits of the Enlightenment myth; or perhaps one should say it is one of the forms this myth takes. It would be interesting to trace the rise of this illusion, through a series of moves that are in part well-founded and in part themselves grounded on illusions. In another essay, I identified three, of which the first two are relatively well traced and the third requires more elaborate description.[18] I'll briefly mention the first two here

First comes 1. foundationalism, which one sees most famously with Descartes. This combines a supposedly indubitable starting point (the particulate ideas in the mind) with an infallible method (that of clear and distinct ideas) and thus should yield conclusions that would live up to claim a. But this comes unstuck—and in two places. The indubitable starting points can be challenged by a determined skepticism, such as we find in Hume, and the method relies much too much on a priori argument and not enough on empirical input.

But even though his foundationalism and his a priori physics were rejected, Descartes left behind α. a belief in the importance of finding the correct method and β. the crucial account which underpins the notion of reason alone. He claimed to be prescinding from all external authority, whether emanating from society or tradition, whether inculcated by parents or teachers, and to rely only on what monological reason can verify as certain. The proper use of reason is sharply distinguished from what we receive from authority. In the Western tradition this supposedly external imposition comes to include, indeed to find its paradigm in, religious revelation. As the Marquis de Condorcet put it, in his account of the progress of the human mind:

Il fut enfin permis de proclamer hautement ce droit si longtemps méconnu de soumettre toutes les opinions à notre propre raison, c'est-à-dire d'employer, pour saisir la vérité, le seul instrument qui nous ait été donné pour la reconnaître. Chaque homme apprit, avec une sorte d'orgueil, que la nature ne l'avait pas absolument destiné à croire sur la parole d'autrui; et la superstition del'Antiquité, l'abaissement de la raison devant le délire d'une foi surnaturelle disparurent de la société comme de la philosophie.[19]

[It was finally permitted to resolutely proclaim this right, so long unrecognized, to submit all opinions to our own reason, that is to say, to employ, for seizing on the truth, the sole instrument that we have been given for recognition. Each man learned, with a certain pride, that his nature was not absolutely destined to believe in the words of others; the superstition of antiquity and the abasement of reason before the delirium of a supernatural faith disappeared from society as from philosophy.]

Our reasoning power is here defined as autonomous and self-sufficient. Proper reason takes nothing on "faith" in any sense of the word. We might call this the principle of "self-sufficient reason." The story of its rise and its self-emancipation comes to be seen as a kind of coming of age of humanity. As Kant put it, not long after Condorcet wrote, Enlightenment is the emergence of human beings from a state of tutelage for which they were themselves responsible, a "selbstbeschuldigte Unmündigkeit" (a self-incurred nonage). The slogan of the age was *sapere aude*! Dare to know.[20]

The first crucial move is that to self-sufficient reason. The second 2. was to point to natural science as a model for the science of society, the move we see in Hobbes, for instance. I shall not pursue this further here because reductive views of social science have less credibility today, although they are, alas, still present on the scene.

This whole matter deserves much further consideration, more than I can give it here. But I am convinced that this further examination would lend even more credibility to the revisionary polysemy I am proposing here, which amounts to this: What deserve to be called secularist regimes in contemporary democracy have to be conceived not primarily as bulwarks against religion but as good faith attempts to secure the three (or four) basic goals I have outlined in this chapter. And this means that they attempt to shape their institutional arrangements not to remain true to hallowed tradition but to maximize the basic goals of liberty and equality between basic beliefs.

NOTES

1. Rajeev Bhargava, "What Is Secularism For?" in Rajeev Bargava, ed., *Secularism and Its Critics* (Delhi: Oxford University Press, 1998), pp. 586–552; see especially pp. 493–494 and 520 for "principled distance"; and "The Distinctiveness of Indian Secularism" in T. N. Srinavasan, ed., *The Future of Secularism* (Delhi: Oxford University Press, 1997), pp. 39–41.

2. José Casanova, "Nativism and the Politics of Gender in Catholicism and Islam," in Hanna Herzog and Ann Braude, eds., *Gendered Modernities: Women, Religion, and Politics* (NY: Palgrave Macmillan, 2009).

3. Andrew Koppelman, personal correspondence.

4. Church of the Holy Trinity v. United States, 143 U.S. 457 at 471.

5. Christian Smith, *The Secular Revolution* (Berkeley: University of California Press, 2003). See also Tisa Wenger, "The God-in-the-Constitution Controversy: American Secularisms in Historical Perspective," in Linell Cady and Elizabeth Shakman Hurd, eds., *Comparative Secularisms in a Global Age* (New York: Palgrave, 2010), 87–106.

6. Marcel Gauchet, *La Religion dans la démocratie* (Paris: Gallimard, 1998), pp. 47–50.

7. Rousseau, who laid bare very early the logic of this idea, saw that a democratic sovereign couldn't just be an "aggregation"; it has to be an "association," that is, a strong collective agency, a "corps moral et collectif" (moral and collective body) with "son unité, son moi commun, sa vie et sa volonté" (its unity, its common self, its life and its will). This last term is the key one, because what gives this body its personality is a "volonté générale" (general will). *Du Contrat Social*, book 1, chapter 6.

8. I have discussed this relation in "Les Sources de l'identité moderne," in Mikhaël Elbaz, Andrée Fortin, and Guy Laforest, eds., *Les Frontières de l'Identité: Modernité et postmodernisme au Québec* (Sainte-Foy: Presses de l'Université Laval, 1996), pp. 347–364.

9. "And it is this symbolic dimension of the fusion of politics and religion for the description of which the concept of 'the political' can properly be used." Jürgen Habermas, "The Political," in this volume, p. 18.

10. See Charles Taylor, *Modern Social Imaginaries* (Durham: Duke University Press, 2004).

11. Jürgen Habermas, *Between Naturalism and Religion* (Cambridge: Polity, 2008), p. 131. Of course, Habermas is right: official language in

diverse democracies must avoid certain religious references (although this shouldn't be stretched to include assembly debates), but this is not because they are specifically religious, but rather because they are not shared. It would be just as unacceptable for, say, legislation to be justified by a "whereas" clause referring to an atheist philosophy as by such a clause referring to the authority of the Bible.

12. I am not sure whether I am disagreeing with Habermas or whether the difference in formulation really amounts to a difference in practice. We both recognize contexts in which the language of the state has to respect a reserve of neutrality and others in which freedom of speech is unlimited. We differ perhaps more in our rationales than in the practice we recommend.

13. Sometimes the obligation of citizens to address their compatriots in the language of secular reason is grounded in an obligation to make one's position intelligible to them. "The self-understanding of the constitutional state has developed within the framework of a contractualist tradition that relies on "natural reason," in other words solely on public arguments to which all persons are supposed to have equal access." Jürgen Habermas, "Religion in the Public Sphere," *European Journal of Philosophy* 14, no. 1 (2006): 5. But what reason is there to think that "natural reason" offered us a kind of ideological Esperanto? Were Martin Luther King's secular compatriots unable to understand what he was arguing for when he put the case for equality in biblical terms? Would more people have got the point had he invoked Kant? And besides, how does one distinguish religious from secular language? Is the Golden Rule clearly a move in either one or the other?

14. Mark Lilla, *The Stillborn God* (New York: Knopf, 2007), p. 5.

15. Ibid., p.162.

16. Ibid., pp. 305–306.

17. Habermas is an exceptional figure; in many respects, of course, but here I want to point out that although he is a major thinker in the epistemological religion/reason distinction (for which I will criticize him), he most emphatically does *not* share the political mistrust of religion that often goes with this.

18. Charles Taylor, "Blosse Vernunft" (forthcoming).

19. Nicolas de Caritat, marquis de Condorcet, *Esquisse d'un tableau historique des progrès de l'esprit humain* (Paris: Flammarion, 1988),

p. 225. I have learned a great deal from the interesting discussion in Vincent Descombes, *Le raisonnement de l'ours* (Paris: Seuil, 2007), pp. 163–178.

20. Immanuel Kant, "Was ist Aufklärung?" in *Kants Werke* (Berlin: Walter de Gruyter, 1968), 13:33.

DIALOGUE

Jürgen Habermas and Charles Taylor

CRAIG CALHOUN: Thank you both, Jürgen and Chuck, for really interesting, challenging discussions. They are similar and connected enough that I think we are discussing a common terrain, and there are enough differences that it ought to be possible to continue discussing it in fruitful ways.

I want to give Jürgen a chance to respond first, having just heard Charles. Let me pose a particular question, to start this.

Part of the burden of Charles's talk was to suggest that religion should not be considered a special case, either with regard to political discourse or with regard to reason and argumentation in general, but, rather, that religion is simply one instance of the more general challenge of diversity, including diversity in comprehensive views of the good, in Rawls's language. Therefore, analogous to the difference between utilitarians and Kantians, we may have the possibly declining difference between Episcopalians and Catholics these days.

Does this make sense to you? Would you buy this argument? If not, does it give you a chance to elaborate your position a little, to clarify why?

JÜRGEN HABERMAS: I think I understand the motivation, but I do not accept the reason that Chuck is here proposing to level a distinction which still seems to me very relevant in our context.

As to the motivation, I would immediately agree that it makes no sense to oppose one sort of reason, secular, against religious reasons on the assumption that religious reasons are coming out of a worldview which is inherently irrational. Reason is working in religious traditions, as well as in any other cultural enterprise, including science. So there is no difference on that broad cultural level of reasoning. At a general cognitive level, there is only one and the same human reason.

However, if it comes to lumping together Kantianism and utilitarianism, Hegelianism and so on with religious doctrines, then I would say there are differences in kind between reasons. One way to put it is that "secular" reasons can be expressed in a "public," or generally shared, language. This is the conventional sense that Chuck is trying to circumvent by introducing the term *official* language.

Anyhow, secular reasons in this sense belong to a context of assumptions—in this case to a philosophical approach, which is distinguished from any kind of religious tradition by the fact that it doesn't require membership in a community of believers. By using any kind of religious reasons, you are implicitly appealing to membership in a corresponding religious community. Only if one is a member and can speak in the first person from within a particular religious tradition does one share a specific kind of experience on which religious convictions and reasons depend.

To put it bluntly, the most important experience—and I'm not ranking it above or below anything else, please—arises from participation in cultic practices, in the actual performance of worshipping in which no Kantian or utilitarian has to participate in order to make a good Kantian or utilitarian argument. So it's a kind of experience that is blocked, so to say, or not taken into account, is abstracted from, once you move in the secular space of giving and taking reasons.

Secular reasons lack links to socialization in a community of one of the four or five great world religions which can be traced back to the historic person of a founder or, more generally, to historical origins. These are traditions that have been continued through the persistent interpretation of a specific doctrine. It depends on such a socialization whether one understands, for example, what it means to appeal to revealed truths. It is difficult to explain what "revelation" means without such a background. If you compare a discussion between Kantians and utilitarians with interreligious debates you face another important difference. Philosophical doctrines are not internally connected with a specific path to salvation. To follow a path to salvation means to follow, in the course of your life, an exemplary figure who draws his authority from ancient sources or testimonies.

A path to salvation is different from any kind of profane ethical life project that an individual person can attribute to herself.

Thus the evidence for religious reasons does not only depend on cognitive beliefs and their semantic nexus with other beliefs, but on existential beliefs that are rooted in the social dimension of membership, socialization, and prescribed practices.

CHARLES TAYLOR: A lot of very interesting points made there. I don't agree with all of them—I don't agree, particularly, about the distinction between ethics and religion. Thomas Aquinas talks about the three theological virtues, which give a different idea of what the good life is.

But anyway, let's leave that aside, because I think the really, really key issue is, what has all that got to do with discourse? If I say something like, "I'm for the rights of human beings because humans were made in the image of God"—that's something that comes out of Genesis—it's not entirely clear right off whether I'm a practicing Jew, a Catholic, a Protestant, or just somebody who thinks that this is a very meaningful thought that came out of Genesis.

I don't see how you can track this in different kinds of discourse—unless we are talking about other kinds of dialogue, where I'm saying to you, "Well, I had this great experience, a vision of the Virgin or St. Therese" and so on. Of course, at that point, that discourse is directly related to this kind of experience. Certain kinds of discourse, if I were trying to describe to you a religious experience, would be directly related to that experience.

But the kind of discourse we're sharing—Martin Luther King had a certain discourse about the U.S. Constitution and its entailments which weren't being followed through. Then he had a very powerful Christian discourse, referring to Exodus, referring to liberation. Nobody had any trouble understanding this. They didn't have to imagine or be able to understand or conceive the deeper experiences that he might have had—the experience in the kitchen, for example, when he decided he had to go on.

How can you discriminate discourses on the basis of the deep psychological background?

I could make another story about the psychological background that Kantians have, and so on, and why they get excited by certain things which don't excite me. But what has that got to do with the discourse out there? Can people not understand it? Why discriminate on those grounds?

HABERMAS: The difference is that religious influences belong to a kind of family of discourse in which you do not just move within a worldview, or within a cognitive interpretation of a domain of human life, but you are speaking out, as I said, from an experience that is tied up with your membership in a community. Talk about being created in God's image is, in our tradition, easily translatable into secular propositions that others derive from the Kantian concept of autonomy or from a certain interpretation of being equipped with human rights.

But translating from one language into the other one does not mean to level the difference between types of reasons. Let me ask you whether I'm right in assuming that behind your strategy of deflating that difference there is a defensive reaction. Do you suspect in the claim to subordinate religious reasons to public reasons in the political decision-making process the attitude of people who find that religious discourse is just not up-to-date, that it's something of the past?

This is not my attitude. What we are doing here, the two of us this afternoon, is that we both are moving in the same space of philosophical and historical or sociological reasoning. Our discourse needs no translation. However, religious speech in the political public sphere needs translation if its content should enter and affect the justification and formulation of binding political decisions that are enforceable by law. In parliaments, courts, or administrative bodies any reference to Genesis 1 should be explained, I think, in secular terms.

TAYLOR: The difference is that I'm saying you can't have translations for those kinds of references because they are the references that really touch on certain people's spiritual lives and not others'. But the same thing goes for the reference to Marx and the reference to Kant. So we are trying to look at not why we have to exclude those references for the purposes of fairness and universality but why these references had to be treated specially—and I still don't understand about the special treatment—because they belong to some kind of different domain.

I certainly agree that there are big, big differences between the reasoning of a deeply religious person about ethics and the reasoning of one who is not. There are certain conceptions of possible human transformation which are believed in by one and not by the other. That's for sure the case.

But there are analogues to this. I can have enough sympathy for the Kantian position, for instance, that I can understand the rhetoric of Kant about "the starry sky above and the moral law within" and *"Achtung für das Gesetz,"* and so on. I can understand that. There's a certain experience behind that. I could imagine somebody saying, "I don't understand what you're talking about. Awe and respect for the law? Are you crazy?" Some people just don't get it.

HABERMAS: I do want to save also the authentic character of religious speech in the public sphere, because I'm convinced that there might well be buried moral intuitions on the part of a secular public that can be uncovered by a moving religious speech. Listening to Martin Luther King, it does make no difference whether you are secular or not. You understand what he means.

This is not a matter on which we differ. Our difference is that, mentioned at least in the essay, there is a call for a "deeper grounding" of constitutional essentials, deeper than that in the secular terms of popular sovereignty and human rights or in "reason alone." This is our difference. There, I think, I cannot follow you because the neutral character of the "official language" you demand for formal political procedures, too, is based on a previous background consensus among citizens, however abstract and vague it may be. Without the presumption of such a consensus on constitutional essentials, citizens of a pluralist society couldn't go to the courts and appeal to specific rights or make arguments by reference to constitutional clauses in the expectation of getting a fair decision.

How can we settle this background consensus in the first place, if not within a space of neutral reasons—and "neutral" now in a peculiar sense. The reasons must be "secular" in a non-Christian sense of "secularization." Let me explain the adjective *non-Christian* in this context. In your book *A Secular Age* you have convincingly described what "secularization" once has meant from within the church. Secularization has had the meaning of tearing down the walls of the monasteries and spreading the radical commands of the Lord across the world without compromise.

But the term *secular* took on a different meaning at the very moment when subjects had to reach a political background consensus across the boundaries of the Christian community—a background consensus in terms of which you can today appeal to a French or German court in order to solve headscarf cases. Those cases must be decided according to procedures and principles that are acceptable for Muslims and their Christian, Jewish, or secular fellow citizens alike. Since the religious legitimation of Christian kings has been substituted with a liberal one, the constitution now provides the source for reasons that are supposed to be shared not only by different religious communities but also by believers and nonbelievers alike. The constitution can provide this common platform only if it in turn can be justified in the light of such reasons that are "secular" in the modern sense. The term *secularization* no longer applies to the universalization of radical beliefs and practices across the Christian world, reaching out from the monastic centers to the profane spheres of everyday social life. Secular reasons do not expand the perspective of one's own community, but push for mutual perspective taking so that different communities can develop a more inclusive perspective by transcending their own universe of discourse. I would like to stick to this usage of the term.

CALHOUN: Let me push back one last time. Then we're going to be almost out of time here on this.

To accent the commonalities here, one of them seems to be that this is all about the capacity for sharing, in some sense, and, from each of you, in a setting where no one has recourse to extradiscursive power. So this is ruling out that set of issues which would involve one set of issues about religion.

It also sounds like, in fact, when Jürgen speaks of religious utterances in the public sphere, that it's not all religious utterances that are at stake and it's not religious motivations, but it's specifically those justifications which are not amenable to being shared because they are based on either cultic experiences, from which many are excluded, or they are based on references to inherently nondiscursive authority, to something outside.

Am I so far fairly characterizing it? So it's not all religious speech. In fact, religious sources for ethics and many other things come in.

But there are certain specific things, and they are problematic precisely if they produce an incapacity to share justifications.

I turn to Charles and ask, conversely, do you think that there is a similar incapacity to share and to discursively resolve the other kinds of differences that you would say are part of the same set with religious differences—cultural differences, ethnic differences, philosophical differences? The claim is going to be that there is the same sort of incapacity, in general, to find fully discursive resolutions or justifications.

TAYLOR: Yes. Think of the history of liberalism. There were attempts by very hard-bitten utilitarians to grab the language in the 1830s. This was what it was going to be all about. Also the people who weren't necessarily religious thought, "This is a takeover. We don't think in those ways."

If you want an emphasis on negotiation, where we put together our charter of rights from different people, it can't be in Benthamite language, it can't be simply in Kantian language, it can't be in Christian language.

What Jürgen calls "secular" I'll call "neutral." That's how I see it. I see it as absolutely indispensable.

CALHOUN: But that doesn't seem to be the heart of the difference. It seems to me that the stronger difference is that, in effect, you are saying that it is impossible to abstract from or prescind from the differences among deep commitments, comprehensive worldviews, etcetera, whether they are grounded religiously or otherwise. So the fundamental discursive issue is that you can't abstract—enough to carry on the discourse and settle things discursively—from any of these kinds of deep constitutive commitments. So religion is not a special case.

I think, to confirm, Jürgen is saying that there are certain specific features that he sees in religious discourse which are more completely excluded from discursive resolution, from sharing in the discursive arena. So, while there might be difficulties getting Kantians and Heideggerians to talk to each other or there might be difficulties getting people of different nationalities to talk to each other, in principle there could be a discursive resolution to the variety of problems that emerge there, but distinctively not for religious problems.

Is that right, Jürgen, or is that going too far?

HABERMAS: I'm, in the first place, maintaining that there are differences in kind between religious and secular reasons. Second, I'm maintaining that religion makes, in view of the historical transition to liberal constitutions, a difference because of the former fusion of religion with politics that had to be in view of the dissolved challenge of religious pluralism. This is the trivial part.

If it comes to a constitution-making discourse or to controversies about the interpretation of special clauses within the frame of an established constitution, I do not think that there are insurmountable obstacles. Religious members of a liberal community would know in advance that certain arguments do not count for those other believing or nonbelieving fellow citizens with whom they are trying to reach an agreement. So they have to be taken from the agenda. This is how I think about developing justice questions and differentiating them from existential, ethical, and religious ones.

CALHOUN: On that level, you're not going to be in strong disagreement, right?

TAYLOR: No, no.

CALHOUN: The disagreement is at another level.

TAYLOR: I just want to tell you one more thing. When we say "religion," we mustn't think of just Christianity. There are Buddhists, there are Hindus. A lot of the things you said don't apply to the other cases at all. That really should give us pause before we make general remarks about—

CALHOUN: Right. This is being argued from within the Western experience. There would need to be a bunch of different discussions within other historical trajectories.

TAYLOR: And they're all here now.

CALHOUN: Indeed they are. And they are us.

IS JUDAISM ZIONISM?

JUDITH BUTLER

I am neither a scholar of religion nor really of public life, but my thinking does intersect with the problem posed here today to the extent that I have been trying in the last years to consider the complex relationship between Judaism, Jewishness, and Zionism, as I know so many other people have as well. My own concern has been to find and foster the patience and perspicacity to think through some issues that seem to be confounded within public discourse. I am not sure whether I have succeeded, but I do know that this is a most difficult and painstaking labor.

I want to say at the outset that we have to be very careful when we refer to "religion" in public life, since finally it may not be possible to talk about "religion" as a category in this sense. Indeed, depending on which religion we have in mind, the relation to the public will be different. There are a variety of religious positions on public life and a variety of ways of conceiving of public life within religious terms. When we begin as we do by asking about "religion" in "public life" we run the risk of simply filling in the category of "religion" with a variety of specific religions, while the sphere of "public life" somehow remains stable, enclosed, and outside of religion. If the entry of religion into public life is a problem, then it would seem that we are presupposing a framework in which religion has been outside public life, and we are asking about how it enters and whether it enters in a justifiable or warranted way. But, if this is the operative assumption, it seems we have to ask first how religion became private and whether the effort to make religion private ever really succeeded. If the implicit question of our inquiry presupposes that religion belongs to a private sphere, we have first to ask which religion has been relegated to the private sphere, and which religions, if any, circulate without question in the public sphere. Perhaps then we might have another inquiry to pursue, namely, one that differentiates between legitimate and illegitimate religions by regulating the distinction between the public and the private. If the public sphere is a Protestant accomplishment, as several scholars have argued, then public life presupposes and reaffirms one dominant religious tradition *as* the secular. And if there are many reasons to doubt whether secularism is as liberated from its religious foundations as it purports to be, we might ask whether these insights into secularism also apply, to some degree, to our claims regarding public life in general. In other words, some religions are not only already "inside" the public sphere, but they help to establish a set of criteria that delimit the public from the private. This happens when some religions are relegated to the "outside"— either as "the private" or as the threat to the public as such—while others function to support and delimit the public sphere itself. If we could not have the distinction between public and private were it not for the Protestant injunction to privatize religion, then religion—or one dominant religious tradition—underwrites the very framework within which we are operating. This would indeed constitute quite a different point of departure for a critical inquiry into religion in public life, since both public and private would form a disjunctive relation that would be, in some important sense, "in" religion from the start.

My point today is not to rehearse the questions about secularism, although I think they have been quite ably expounded by Talal Asad, Saba Mahmood, Michael Warner, Janet Jakobsen, and also by Charles Taylor in his recent work. I do want to suggest that secularization may be a fugitive way for religion to survive, and that we always have to ask which form and path of secularization we mean. My first point is that any generalizations we make about "religion" in "public life" are suspect from the start if we do not think about which religions are being presupposed in the conceptual apparatus itself, and if that conceptual apparatus, including the notion of the public, is not understood in the light of its own genealogy. It makes a different kind of sense to refer to a secular Jew than to a secular Catholic; while both may be presumed to have departed from religious belief, there may be other forms of belonging that do not presume or require belief; secularization may well be one way that Jewish life continues as Jewish. We also make a mistake if religion becomes equated with belief, and belief is then tied to certain kinds of speculative claims about God—a theological presumption that does not always work to describe religious practice. That effort to distinguish the cognitive status of religious and nonreligious belief misses the fact that very often religion functions as a matrix of subject formation, an embedded framework for valuations, and a mode of belonging and embodied social practice. Of course, the legal principle of the separation of state and religion haunts any and all of our discourses here, but there are many reasons to think that that juridical conception cannot sufficiently to serve as the framework for understanding the larger questions of religion in public life. And neither can the debates about religious symbols and icons that have produced widespread disagreement about First Amendment rights, on the one hand, and the protection of religious minorities against discrimination and persecution, on the other hand.[1]

I want to enter this fray with another problem, namely, the tension that emerges between religion and public life when public criticism of Israeli state violence is taken to be anti-Semitic or anti-Jew-ish. For the record, I would like to make clear that some of those criticisms do employ anti-Semitic rhetoric and arguments and do en-gage anti-Semitic sentiment, although many of those criticisms also do not—especially, but not exclusively, those that emerge from within Jewish frameworks of social justice. My aim here is not to distinguish between these two kinds of criticism, although I think they must be distinguished, but to consider whether the public criti-cism of state violence—and I know that term is yet to be explained—is in some sense a Jewish thing to do. You will, I hope, forgive my initial flippancy here, but you will see the quandary I am trying to approach if you consider that if one openly and publicly criticizes Israeli state violence one is then considered anti-Semitic or anti-Jewish, and yet to openly and publicly criticize such violence is in some ways an obligatory ethical demand from within Jewish frame-works, both religious and nonreligious. Of course, you will already see a second set of quandaries introduced by this formulation. As Hannah Arendt made clear in her early writings, Jewishness is not always the same as Judaism.[2] And, as she made clear in her evolving political position on the state of Israel, neither Judaism nor Jewish-ness necessarily leads to the embrace of Zionism.

My aim is not to repeat the claim that Jews differ among them-selves on the value of Zionism, on the injustice of the occupation, or on the military destructiveness of the Israeli state. These are complex matters, and there are vast disagreements on all of them. And my point is not to say simply that Jews are obligated to criticize Israel, although in fact I think they are—we are—given that Israel acts in the name of the Jewish people, casts itself as the legitimate represen-tative of the Jewish people; there is a question as to what is done in the name of the Jewish people and so all the more reason to reclaim that tradition and ethics in favor of another politics. The effort to establish the presence of progressive Jews runs the risk of remaining within certain identitarian presumptions; one opposes any and all expressions of anti-Jewish anti-Semitism and one reclaims Jewishness for a project that seeks to dismantle Israeli state violence. This particular form of the solution is challenged, however, if we consider that, within several ethical frameworks, Jewishness is itself an anti-identitarian project insofar as we might even say that being a Jew implies taking up an ethical relation to the non-Jew. Indeed, if a relevant Jewish tradition for waging public criticism of Israeli state violence is one that draws upon cohabitation as a norm of sociality, then what follows is the need *not only* to establish an alternative Jewish public presence (distinct from AIPAC, for instance) or an alternative Jewish movement (such as Jewish Voice for Peace, for instance), but to affirm the displacement of identity that Jewishness is, as paradoxical as that may sound. Only then can we come to understand the mode of ethical relationality that informs some key historical and religious understandings of what it is to "be" a Jew. In the end, it is not about specifying the ontology of the Jew over and against some other cultural or religious group—we have every reason to be suspect of any effort to do such a thing. It is rather a question of understanding the very relation to the non-Jew as the way of configuring religion in public life within Judaism. And it is on the basis of this conception of cohabitation that the critique of illegitimate nation-state violence can and must be waged.

There are, of course, both risks and obligations in public criticism. It remains true that the criticism of Israeli state violence, for instance, can be construed either as a critique of the Jewish state on the same grounds that one would criticize any other state engaging in the same practices of occupation, invasion, and the destruction of a livable infrastructure for a minority population, or it can be construed as the critique of the Jewish state, emphasizing the Jewishness of that state and raising the question of whether it is because the state is *Jewish* that it is criticized. This, in turn, raises the question of whether the criticism emerges because the state insists on one religious and ethnic group maintaining a demographic majority and creates differential levels of citizenship for majority and minority populations (and even internally prizes Ashkenazi origins and narrative accounts of the nation over Sephardic and Mizrachi cultural origins). Now if the problem is this last one, it is still hard to enunciate this in public, since there will be those who suspect that really something else is being said or that anyone who calls into question the demand for Jewish demographic majority in particular is motivated by insensitivity to the sufferings of the Jewish people, including the contemporary threat they experience, or by outright anti-Semitism or both.

And, of course, it makes a difference whether one is criticizing the principles of Jewish sovereignty that characterize political Zionism since 1948, or whether one's criticism is restricted to the occupation as illegal and destructive (and so situates itself in a history that starts with 1967), or whether one is more restrictively criticizing certain military actions in isolation from both Zionism and the occupation, i.e., last year's assault on Gaza and the war crimes committed there, the growth of settlements, or the policies of the current right-wing regime in Israel. But, in each and every case, there is a question of whether the public criticism can be registered as something other than an attack on the Jews or on Jewishness. Depending on where we are and to whom we speak, some of these positions can be heard more easily than others. And yet, in every case, we are confronted with the limits on audibility by which the contemporary public sphere is constituted. There is always a question: should I listen to this or not? Am I being heard, or misconstrued? The public sphere is constituted time and again through certain kinds of exclusions: images that cannot be seen, words that cannot be heard. And this means that the regulation of the visual and audible field—along with the other senses, to be sure—is crucial to the constitution of what can become a debatable issue within the sphere of politics.[3]

If one says that one would be opposed to any state that restricted full citizenship to any religious or ethnic group at the expense of indigenous populations and all other coinhabitants, then one might well be charged with not understanding the exceptional and singular character of the state of Israel and, more importantly, the historical reasons for claiming that exception. In effect, the formulation of classically liberal principles of citizenship that would forbid discrimination on the basis of race, religion, and ethnicity, for example, are construed as "destructive" of the Jewish state and if that formulation then resounds with "destruction of the Jewish people," especially under those conditions where the Jewish state claims to represent the Jewish people, then this view implicitly establishes classical liberalism as a form of genocide.

The charge that "such views lead to the destruction of the Jewish state" illicitly draws upon the claim that "these views lead to the destruction of the Jewish people" or, more elliptically, "the Jews." But it is clearly one thing to ask about the conditions under which Jews might live peaceably and productively with non-Jews, and to think about forms of governmental authority that might require a transition from the current form of government to another, and quite another to call for the violent destruction of a state or violence against its population. Indeed, the call to rethink federal authority or binationalism for the region as a way of politically embodying principles of cohabitation may well be a way to envisage a way out of violence rather than a path to the destruction of any of the populations on that land.

I think one has to return to certain diasporic traditions within Judaism in order not only to produce a public polyvalence for Jewishness that would effectively contest the right of Israel to exclusively represent Jewish interests, values, or politics but also to reanimate certain ideals of cohabitation. Cohabitation forms the ethical basis for a public critique of those forms of state violence that seek to produce and maintain the Jewish character of the state through the radical disenfranchisement and decimation of its minority, through occupation, assault, or legal restriction. These are attacks on a subjugated minority, but they are also attacks on the value of cohabitation. So what do I mean by this term? Surely it implies something more robust than the claim that we all ought to get along or that neighborliness is a good idea.

I'd like to turn now, briefly, to thinking about Hannah Arendt, Jewish to be sure, but someone whose political views made many people doubt the authenticity of her Jewishness. Indeed, as a result of her salient criticisms of political Zionism and the state of Israel in 1944, '48, and '62, her claim to belong to the Jewish people was severely challenged, most famously by Gershom Scholem.[4] Scholem quickly embraced a conception of political Zionism, whereas Martin Buber in the teens and twenties actively and publicly defended a spiritual and cultural Zionism that, in his early view, would become "perverted" if it assumed the form of a political state. By the 1940s, Arendt, Buber, and Nudah Magnes argued in favor of a binational state, proposing a federation in which Jews and Arabs would maintain their respective cultural autonomy; of course, there are other versions of binationalism that do not presume the monolithic cultural integrity of "two peoples" as Buber did, and I hope to gesture toward that at the end of my remarks. It is worth noting as well that Franz Rosenzweig also elaborated a diasporic opposition to Zionism in his *The Star of Redemption*, in which he argues that Judaism is fundamentally bound up with waiting and wandering but not with the claim of territory.

It was to this diasporic version of Jewishness that Edward Said also referred in his *Freud and the Non-European,* in which he remarks that both Palestinians and Jews have an overlapping history of displacement, exile, living as refugees in diaspora, among those who are not the same. This is a mode of living in which alterity is constitutive of who one is. And it is on the basis of these overlapping senses of the displacement and heterogeneous cohabitation that Said proposes diaspora as a historical resource and guiding principle for a rethinking what a just polity might be for those lands. Of course, there are distinctions to be made between diaspora and exile, especially since Zionists have very often recast diasporic traditions as exilic in order to make the case for an inevitable "return." We see this most clearly in debates about the status of the *galut*, the Jewish population living outside of Israel, who are cast by some Zionists as illegitimate representatives of Judaism. Clearly, Said means something different by referring to both Jews and Palestinians as exilic. His formulation precipitates the question: how does the convergence of histories constitute one meaning for cohabitation?

Said did not clarify in exactly what way these traditions of exile might be overlapping, but he was careful not to draw strict analogies. Does this suggest that one history might inform or interrupt another in ways that call for something other than comparison, parallelism, and analogy? Were Buber and Arendt thinking about a similar problem when, for instance, mindful of the massive numbers of refugees after the Second World War, they expressed their concerns about the establishment of a Jewish state in 1948 that would be based on the disenfranchisement and expulsion of Arabs as a national minority—one that turned out to expel more than seven hundred thousand Palestinians from their rightful homes. Arendt refused any strict historical analogy between the displacement of the Jews from Europe and those of the Palestinians from a newly established Israel; she surveyed a number of historically distinct situations of statelessness to develop the general critique of the nation-state in *The Origins of Totalitarianism* in 1951. There she attempted to show how, for structural reasons, the nation-state produces mass numbers of refugees and *must* produce them in order to maintain the homogeneity of the nation it seeks to represent, in other words, to support the nationalism of the nation-state. This led her to oppose any state formation that sought to reduce or refuse the heterogeneity of its population, including the founding of Israel on principles of Jewish sovereignty, and it is clearly one reason she reflected on the postsovereign and postnational promise of federalism. She thought that any state that failed to have the popular support of all its inhabitants and that defined citizenship on the basis of religious or national belonging would be forced to produce a permanent class of refugees; the critique extended to Israel, which, she thought, would find itself in endless conflict (thus heightening the danger to itself) and would perpetually lack legitimacy as a democracy grounded in a popular will, especially in light of its continued reliance on "superpowers" to maintain its political power in the region. That Arendt moved from an analysis of a series of stateless conditions to a consideration of Palestine as a stateless condition is significant. The centrality of the European refugee situation both under fascist Germany and after its demise informs her politics here. But this is certainly *not* to say that Zionism is Nazism. Arendt would have refused such an equation, as we must too. The point is that there are principles of social justice that can be derived from the Nazi genocide that can and must inform our contemporary struggles, even though the contexts are different, and the forms of subjugating power clearly distinct.

I mean to suggest that cohabitation may be understood as a form of convergent exiles but that we are mistaken if we imagine this convergence has to take the form of strict analogy. If Edward Said made the claim that the exilic condition of both Palestinian and Jewish people makes for a convergence without analogy, Arendt made it differently when she wrote that the conditions of statelessness under the Nazi regime require a larger critique of how the nation-state perpetually produces the problem of mass refugees. She did not say that the historical situation under Nazi Germany was the same as the situation in Israel. Not at all. But the former was part—not all—of what led her to develop a historical account of statelessness in the twentieth century and to derive general principles that oppose the condition that produce stateless persons and persons without rights. In some ways she invoked the repetition of statelessness as the condition from which a critique of the nation-state has to take place, in the name of heterogeneous populations, political plurality, and a certain conception of cohabitation. It is clear that Jewish history comes to bear on Palestinian history through the impositions and exploitations of a project of settler colonialism. But is there yet another mode in which these histories come to bear upon one another, one that sheds another kind of light?

Although I think there are some religious sources for Arendt's political thought, I understand that I am a minority in this regard. It is clear that her early work on Augustine, for instance, focuses on neighborly love.[5] And in the early writings on Zionism she seeks recourse to the famous formulation of Hillel, "If I am not for myself, who will be for me? If I am not for others, what am I? And if not now, when?" In 1948 she wrote an essay, "Jewish History, Revised," in which she assesses the importance of Scholem's *Major Trends in Jewish Mysticism*, published two years earlier. There she considers the importance of the messianic tradition for establishing the notion of God as "impersonal" and "infinite" and as linked less with stories of creation than with accounts of *emanation*. Commenting on the "esoteric character" of such mystical ideas, Arendt underscores that a more important legacy of mysticism is the notion that humans participate in the powers that shape the "drama of the world," thus delineating a sphere of action for humans who saw themselves as obligated to a broader purpose. As messianic hopes proved less credible and legal exegesis less efficacious, this resolution of the mystical tradition into a form of action became more important. But this idea of action depended on the exilic existence of the Jewish people, a point explicitly made by Isaac Luria, whom Arendt cites: "Formerly [the diaspora] had been regarded either as a punishment for Israel's sins or as a test of Israel's faith. Now it still is all this, but intrinsically it is a mission; its purpose is to uplift the fallen sparks from all their various locations."[6] To uplift the fallen sparks is not to gather them again or to return them to their origin. What interests Arendt is not only the irreversibility of "emanation" or dispersal but the revalorization of exile that it implies. Is there then, perhaps, also a way to understand that the embrace of heterogeneity is itself a certain diasporic position, one conceptualized in part through the notion of scattered population? The kabbalistic tradition of scattered light, of the *sephirot*, articulated this notion of a divine scattering that presupposes the dwelling of Jews among non-Jews.

Although Arendt scorned explicitly political forms of messianism, the exilic tradition from which and about which she wrote was also bound up with a certain version of the messianic, one that interested her, for instance, in Benjamin's reading of Kafka. Over and against the messianic version of history that Scholem later adopted, which provided a redemptive historical narrative for the establishment of the state of Israel, Arendt was clearly closer to Benjamin's counter-messianic view. In that view, it was the suffering of the oppressed that flashed up during moments of emergency and that interrupted both homogeneous and teleological time. Here I agree with Gabriel Piterberg's argument that, over and against Scholem, who finally understood the messianic as implying a return of the Jews to the land of Israel, which Scholem understood as a return *from* exile *to* history, Benjamin's "Theses 'On the Concept of History'" constituted "an ethical and political drive to redeem humanity's oppressed."[7] As an effort to reverse the devalorization of "exile" (and *galut*) within Zionist historiography, several scholars, including Amnon Raz-Krakotzin,[8] focus their reading of Benjamin on the recognition and remembrance of the dispossessed. No one people could claim a monopoly on dispossession. The exilic framework for understanding the messianic provides a way to understand one historical condition of dispossession in light of another. Forms of national historiography that presuppose an internal history of the Jews are able to understand neither the exilic condition of the Jews nor the exilic consequences for the Palestinian under contemporary Zionism.[9] Redemption itself is to be rethought as the exilic, without return, a disruption of teleological history and an opening to a convergent and interruptive set of temporalities. This is a messianism, perhaps secularized, that affirms the scattering of light, the exilic condition, as the nonteleological form that redemption now takes. This is a redemption, then, from teleological history. But how, we might surely ask, does the remembrance of one exile prompt an attunement or opening to the dispossession of another? What is this transposition? Can it be something other than historical analogy? And how does it take us to another notion of cohabitation?

Raz-Krakotzin writes that the tradition of Benjamin's *Theses* does not mobilize the memory of the oppression of the Jews in order to legitimate the particularist claims of the present, but serves as a catalyst for building a more general history of oppression; this generalization and transposability of that history of oppression is what leads to a politics that also generalizes a commitment to alleviating oppression.

Although Arendt clearly rejected all messianic versions of history, it is clear that her own resistance to the progress narrative of political Zionism was formed in part within terms offered by Benjamin. In her introduction to Benjamin's *Illuminations*, Arendt remarks that in the early 1920s Benjamin turned to baroque tragic drama, a move that seemed to parallel, if not draw upon, Scholem's turn to the Kabbalah. Arendt suggests that, throughout this work, Benjamin affirms there to be no "return," whether to German, European, or Jewish traditions in their former condition. And yet something from Judaism, namely the exilic tradition, articulates this impossibility of return. Instead, something of another time flashes up in our own. Arendt writes that there was in Benjamin's work of this time "an implicit admission that the past spoke directly only through things that had been handed down, whose seeming closeness to the present was thus due precisely to their exotic [exoteric? esoteric?] character, which ruled out all claims to a binding authority." She understood as "theologically inspired" Benjamin's conclusion that the truth could not be directly recovered and so could not be "an unveiling which destroys the secret, but the revelation that does it justice."[10]

The revelation that does the secret justice does not seek to recover an original meaning or to return to a lost past, but rather to grasp and work with the fragments of the past that break through into a present where they become provisionally available. This view seems to find resonance in that remark in the "Theses 'On the Concept of History'" that "the true picture of the past flits by. The past can be seized only as an image which flashes up at the instant when it can be recognized and is never seen again." Or, later: "to articulate the past historically does not mean to recognize it 'the way it really was.' It means to seize hold of a memory as it flashes up at a moment of danger. . . . The Messiah comes not only as the redeemer, but as the subduer of the Antichrist." The Messiah is neither a person nor a historical event; it can be understood neither as anthropomorphism nor as teleology; rather, it is a memory of suffering from another time that interrupts and reorients the politics of this time. It is memory that takes momentary shape as a form of light, recalling the kabbalistic *sephirot*, those scattered and quasi-angelic illuminations that break up the suspect continuity of the present along with its amnesia. Benjamin makes clear in the seventeenth thesis that this flashing up makes possible a pause within a historical development, a "cessation of happening" that can produce "a revolutionary chance in the fight for the oppressed past." A certain breaking apart of the amnesiac surface of time, then, opens onto, and transposes, the memory of suffering into the future of justice, not as revenge but as the figuring of a time in which the history that covers over the history of oppression might cease.[11]

In order to return us to the problem of how best to think about cohabitation, let me remind you of Arendt's famous final accusation against Eichmann in her controversial book, *Eichmann in Jerusalem*, published in 1962.[12] According to Arendt, Eichmann thought that he and his superiors *might choose* with whom to cohabit the earth and failed to realize that the heterogeneity of the earth's population is an irreversible condition of social and political life itself.

The accusation bespeaks a firm conviction that none of us should be in the position of making such a choice, that those with whom we cohabit the earth are given to us, prior to choice, and so prior to any social or political contracts we might enter through deliberate volition. In fact, if we seek to make a choice where there is no choice, we are trying to destroy the conditions of our own social and political life. In Eichmann's case the effort to choose with whom to cohabit the earth was an explicit effort to annihilate some part of that population—Jews, gypsies, homosexuals, communists, the disabled and the ill, among others—and so the exercise of freedom upon which he insisted was genocide. If Arendt is right, then it is not only that we may not choose with whom to cohabit but that we must actively preserve the nonchosen character of inclusive and plural cohabitation: we not only live with those we never chose, and to whom we may feel no social sense of belonging, but we are also obligated to preserve those lives and the plurality of which they form a part. In this sense, concrete political norms and ethical prescriptions emerge from the unchosen character of these modes of cohabitation. To cohabit the earth is prior to any possible community or nation or neighborhood. We might choose where to live, and who to live by, but we cannot choose with whom to cohabit the earth.

In *Eichmann in Jerusalem* Arendt clearly speaks not only for the Jews but also for any other minority who would be expelled from habitation on the earth by another group. The one implies the other, and the "speaking for" universalizes the principle even as it does not override the plurality for which it speaks. Arendt refuses to separate the Jews from the other so-called nations persecuted by the Nazis in the name of a plurality that is coextensive with human life in any and all its cultural forms. Is she subscribing here to a universal principle, or does plurality form a substantial alternative to the universal? And is her procedure related to the problem of convergent and interrupting histories mentioned by both Said and Benjamin in different ways?

Perhaps we can say there is a universalization at work in Arendt's formulation that seeks to establish inclusiveness for all human society, but one that posits no single defining principle for the humanity it assembles. This notion of plurality cannot be only *internally* differentiated, since that would raise the question of what bounds this plurality; that boundary would establish not only an inside but an outside, and since plurality cannot be exclusionary without losing its plural character, the idea of a given or established form for plurality would pose a problem for the claims of plurality. It is clear that for Arendt, nonhuman life already constitutes part of that outside, thus denying from the start the animality of the human. Any present notion of the human will have to be differentiated on some basis from a future one. If plurality does not exclusively characterize a given and actual condition, but also always a potential one, then it has to be understood as a process, and we will need to shift from a static to a dynamic conception.

Following William Connolly, we could then speak of *pluralization*.[13] Only then can the differentiation that characterizes a given plurality also mark that set of differences that exceeds its givenness. The task of affirming or even safeguarding plurality would then also imply making new modes of pluralization possible. When Arendt universalizes her claim (no one has the right to decide with whom to cohabit the earth; everyone has the right to cohabit the earth with equal degrees of protection), she does not assume that "everyone" is the same—at least not in the context of her discussion of plurality. One can surely see why there would be a Kantian reading of Arendt, one that concludes that plurality is a regulative ideal, that everyone has such rights, regardless of the cultural and linguistic differences by which anyone is characterized. And Arendt herself moves in this Kantian direction, but mainly through the extrapolation of Kant's notion of aesthetic judgment rather than his moral philosophy.

There is, however, another important point to be made here, one that honors the distinction between pluralization and universalization and upholds that distinction as important for thinking about unchosen cohabitation. Equal protection or, indeed, equality, is not a principle that homogenizes those to whom it applies; rather, the commitment to equality is a commitment to the process of differentiation itself. One can surely see why there can be a communitarian reading of Arendt, since she herself elaborates the right to belong and rights of belonging. But there is always a redoubling here that dislocates the claim from any specific community: *everyone* has the right of belonging. And this means there is a universalizing and a differentiating that takes place at once and without contradiction— and that this is in fact the structure of pluralization. In other words, political rights are separated from the social ontology upon which they depend; political rights universalize, but always in the context of a differentiated (and continually differentiating) population. And though Arendt refers to "nations" or sometimes communities of belonging as the component parts of this plurality, it is clear that the principle of pluralization also applies to these parts themselves, since they are not only internally differentiated (and differentiating), but are themselves defined in terms of variable and shifting relations to the outside.

Indeed, this is one point I have been underscoring about the problem of Jewishness. It may be that the sense of belonging to that group entails taking up a relation to the non-Jew and that this mode of approaching the problem of alterity is fundamental to what it is to "belong" to Jewishness itself.[14] In other words, to belong is to undergo a dispossession from the category, as paradoxical as that might seem. Although Arendt herself values the way that exile leads to action in the service of broader purposes, here we might read dispossession as an exilic moment, one that disposes us ethically. Paradoxically, it is only possible to struggle to alleviate the suffering of others if I am both motivated and dispossessed by my own suffering. It is this relation to the other that dispossesses me from any enclosed and self-referential notion of belonging; otherwise we cannot understand those obligations that bind us when there is no obvious mode of belonging, where the convergence of temporalities becomes the condition for the memory of political dispossession as well as the resolve to bring such dispossession to a halt.

Can we now think about the transposition that happens from the past to the future? Precisely because there is *no* common denominator among the plural members of this stipulated humanity, except perhaps the ungrounded right to have rights, which includes a certain right to belonging and to place, we could only begin to understand this plurality by testing a set of analogies that will invariably fail. In fact, precisely because one historical experience of dispossession is not the same as another, the right to have rights emerges invariably in different forms and through different vernaculars. If we start with the presumption that one group's suffering is *like* another group's, we have not only assembled the groups into provisional monoliths, we have also launched into a form of analogy building that will invariably fail. The specificity of the group is established at the expense of its temporal and spatial instability, its constitutive heterogeneity, for the purpose of making it suitable for analogical reasoning. But analogy fails because the specificities prove obdurate. The suffering of one people is not exactly like the suffering of another, and this is the condition of the specificity of the suffering for both. Indeed, we would have no analogy between them if the grounds for analogy were not already destroyed. And if specificity qualifies each group for analogy, it also defeats the analogy from the start.

The obstruction that thwarts analogy makes that specificity plain and becomes the condition for the process of pluralization. Through elaborating a series of such broken, or exhausted, analogies, the communitarian presumption that we might start with "groups" as our point of departure meets its limit, and then the internally and externally differentiating action of pluralization emerges as a clear alternative. We might try to overcome such "failures" by devising more perfect analogies, hoping that a common ground can be achieved in that way ("multicultural dialogue" with an aim of perfect consensus or intersectional analysis in which every factor is included in the final picture). But such procedures miss the point that plurality implies differentiations, which cannot be (and should not be) overcome through ever more robust epistemological accounts or refined analogies. At the same time, the elaboration of rights, especially the right of cohabitation on the earth, emerges as a universal that governs a social ontology that cannot be homogenized. Such a universalizing right has to break up into its nonuniversal conditions; otherwise, it fails to be grounded in plurality.

Arendt seeks something other than principles to unify this plurality, and she clearly objects to any effort to divide this plurality, although it is, by definition, internally differentiated. The difference between division and differentiation is clear: it is one thing to *repudiate* some part of this plurality, to bar admission of that part into the plurality of the human, and to deny place to that portion of humanity. And it is another to recognize the failed analogies by which we have to make our way politically. One suffering is never the same as another. At the same time, any and all suffering by virtue of forcible displacement and statelessness is equally unacceptable.

If we are to allow the memory of dispossession to crack the surface of historical amnesia and reorient us toward the unacceptable conditions of refugees across time and context, there must be transposition without analogy, the interruption of one time by another, which is the counternationalist impetus of the messianic in Benjamin's terms, what some would call a messianic secularism. One time breaks into another precisely when that former time was to remain forgotten for all time. This is not the same as the operation of analogy, but neither is it the same as the temporality of trauma. In trauma the past is never over; in historical amnesia the past never was, and that "never was" becomes the condition of the present.

It may be that the very possibility of ethical relation depends upon a certain condition of dispossession from national modes of belonging, a dispossession that characterizes our relationality from the start, and so the possibility of any ethical relation. We are outside ourselves, before ourselves, and only in such a mode is there a chance of being for another. We are, to be sure, already in the hands of the other before we make any decision about with whom we choose to live. This way of being bound to one another is precisely *not* a social bond that is entered into through volition and deliberation; it precedes contract, is mired in dependency, and is often effaced by those forms of social contract that depend on an ontology of volitional individuality. Thus it is, even from the start, to the stranger that we are bound, the one, or the ones, we never knew and never chose. If we accept this sort of ontological condition, then to destroy the other is to destroy my life, that sense of my life that is invariably social life. This may be less our common condition than our convergent condition—one of proximity, adjacency, up againstness, one of being interrupted by the memory of someone else's longing and suffering, in spite of oneself. Since there is no home without adjacency, and no way to reside anywhere without the outside defining the space of inhabitation, the *co* of *cohabitation* cannot be thought simply as spatial neighborliness. There is dependency and differentiation, proximity and violence; this is what we find in some explicit ways in the relation between territories, such as Israel and Palestine, since they are joined inextricably, without binding contract, without reciprocal agreement, and yet ineluctably. So the question emerges: what obligations are to be derived from this dependency, contiguity, and proximity that now defines each population, that exposes each to the fear of destruction, which, as we know, sometimes incites destructiveness? How are we to understand such bonds, without which neither population can live and survive? To what postnational obligations do they lead?

Practically, I think none of these questions can be dissociated from the critique of the ongoing and violent project of settler colonialism that constitutes political Zionism. To practice remembrance in the Benjaminian sense might lead to a new concept of citizenship, a new constitutional basis for that region, a rethinking of binationalism in light of the racial and religious complexity of both Jewish and Palestinian populations, a radical reorganization of land partitions and illegal property allocations, and even, minimally, a concept of cultural heterogeneity that extends to the entire population, which is protected rather than denied by rights of citizenship. Now, one might argue, against all these propositions, that they are unreasonable to speak in public, that they carry too much risk, that equality would be bad for the Jews, that democracy would stoke anti-Semitism, and that cohabitation would threaten Jewish life with destruction. But perhaps such responses are only utterable on the condition that we fail to remember what Jewish means or that we have not thought carefully enough about all the possible permutations of "never again"; after all, remembrance does not restrict itself to my suffering or the suffering of my people alone. The limit on what can be remembered is enforced in the present through what can be said and what can be heard—the limits of the audible and the sensible that constitute the public sphere. For remembrance to break through into that public sphere would be one way for religion, perhaps, to enter into public life one way to conceive of a politics, Jewish and not Jewish—indeed one not restricted to that binary—extending, as it must, to a field of open differentiation uncontained by the universalization that it supports. This politics might emerge in the name of remembrance, both from and against dispossession, and in the direction of what may yet be called justice.

NOTES

1. See Talal Asad, Wendy Brown, Judith Butler, and Saba Mahmood, *Is Critique Secular?* (Berkeley: University of California Press, 2009).

2. Hannah Arendt, *The Origins of Totalitarianism* (New York: Hartcourt Brace Jovanovich, 1951), p. 66; *Rachel Varnhagen: The Life of a Jewish Woman* (New York: Harcourt Brace Jovanovich, 1974), pp. 216–228.

3. See Jacques Rancière on the "distribution of the sensible" in *The Politics of Aesthetics: The Distribution of the Sensible*, trans. Gabriel Rockhill (New York: Continuum, 2004).

4. Arendt emerged from a complex tradition of German-Jewish thought, and I do not mean to engage in an idealization here, since there are many reasons *not* to idealize her. She articulated some clearly racist beliefs and she is no model for a broader politics of understanding across cultural difference. But she continues a German-Jewish debate that began in the late nineteenth century about the value and meaning of Zionism. There was, for instance, a famous debate between Hermann Cohen, the neo-Kantian Jewish philosopher, and Gershom Scholem on the value of Zionism in which Cohen criticized the nascent nationalism of Zionism and offered instead a vision of the Jewish people as cosmopolitan or "hyphenated." Cohen argued that Jews were best served by becoming part of the German nation—a view that could only prove most painful and impossible in light of the development of German fascism and its virulent anti-Semitism. Arendt shared Cohen's high valuation of German culture, though she rejected that nationalism.

5. Hannah Arendt, *Love and Saint Augustine*, ed. Joanna Vecchiarelli Scott and Judith Chelius Stark (Chicago: University of Chicago Press, 2007).

6. Cited in *The Jewish Writings: Hannah Arendt*, ed. Jerome Kohn and Ron H. Feldman (New York: Schocken, 1997), p. 309.

7. Gabriel Piterberg, *The Returns of Zionism* (London: Verso, 2008).

8. Amnon Raz-Krakotzin, "Jewish Memory Between Exile and History," *Jewish Quarterly Review* 97, no. 4 (Fall 2007): 530–543; "Exile Within Sovereignty: Toward a Critique of the 'Negation of Exile' in Israeli Culture," part 1, *Theory and Criticism* [Hebrew] 4 (Autumn 1993): 23–56; part 2, *Theory and Criticism* 5 (1994): 113–132; *Exil et souveraineté* (Paris: La Fabrique, 2007).

9. Of course, as Arendt herself points out, the need to establish an "internal" history of the Jewish people is one way to counter the position, held by Sartre and others, that the historical life of the Jews is determined mainly or exclusively by anti-Semitism.

10. Walter Benjamin, *Illuminations* (New York: Schocken, 1968), pp. 40–41.

11. This raises a complex question about the relation between the "cessation of happening" characteristic of the general strike and the end to a homogeneous form of history. At what point does the first cessation become the condition for the second, or are they at some point continuous with one another?

12. Hannah Arendt, *Eichmann in Jerusalem* (New York: Schocken, 1963), pp. 277–278.

13. William Connolly, *The Ethos of Pluralization* (Minneapolis: University of Minnesota Press, 2005).

14. See Emmanuel Levinas, *Otherwise Than Being, or, Beyond Essence* trans. A. Lingis (Dordrecht: Kluwer, 1978).

PROPHETIC RELIGION AND THE FUTURE OF CAPITALIST CIVILIZATION

CORNEL WEST

It was almost forty years ago when I first read *Knowledge and Human Interests*, and it changed my life. It was the first philosophic text that I gave a public presentation on at Princeton. To be able now to be in a dialogue with Professor Habermas is, in fact, more than a blessing. It's true I was blessed to sit in his seminar in Frankfurt in 1987, with Roberto Unger and Thomas McCarthy, who is here, a towering figure in his own right. But to be part of this dialogue, for me, is very, very special.

The same holds for Charles Taylor here. I was blessed to be part of a dialogue at Cardozo Law School maybe twenty years ago, wrestling with Hegel and Critical Legal Studies. To have him back in New York and to have me be a part of this gets me excited, even though I have a cold. I apologize for that.

Of course, Judith Butler is the leading social theorist of our generation.

So when you have the towering European philosopher in the house, the towering North American philosopher, and the leading social theorist, and a blues man like me, we're going to have a good time.

That's how I come to you tonight, as a blues man in the life of the mind, a jazzman in the world of ideas. What I mean by that is this.

I want to begin with some stage setting. I want to begin with a metaphilosophic note. Let's go back to line 607b5 in the tenth book of Plato's *Republic*, the traditional quarrel between philosophy and poetry, and Plato's attempt to displace Homer, for the first time in Western civilization, to create a space for something called "love of wisdom" in a systematic way. People had been loving wisdom for a long time before that. But now Plato says there is a way of generating a space in the culture for something called philosophy, and it must displace poetry.

Well, you see, as a blues man, I believe philosophy must go to school with poetry. When Beethoven called himself a poet of tones when he walked with Goethe, it included musicians. I take quite seriously the last line of Shelley's great pamphlet *A Defence of Poetry*: "Poets are the unacknowledged legislators of the world." What he meant was that poets are not simply versifiers; they are all of us who have the courage to muster empathy and imagination in the face of the chaos that we find ourselves in, to create and use bits of the world in order to change the world in light of a new vision of the world.

So, in that way, when we are talking about rethinking secularism, we have to think of the ways in which secular thinkers—namely, those who go to school with science such as Brother Christopher Hitchens, must become more religiously musical. Too many secular thinkers are religiously tone-deaf and flat-footed.

But it cuts the other way, too. Religious persons like myself must be secularly musical, because, through empathy and imagination, we must try to get inside other peoples' view of the world, to understand why persons are convinced by this set of arguments, these kinds of reasons as to why they are agnostic or why they're atheistic or what have you. It's no small thing. Very fragile experiments in democracy could well depend on not just the character and virtue of the citizens but also the ability to be multicontextual in the various frameworks and reason-giving activities in public spaces.

It's not as if there's not conflict in those private spaces either. You go to a synagogue in the evening and watch that fascinating interpretive conflict take place over the Torah. There's an overarching agreement on its revelatory status—despite intense disagreement on what it means. How do we mediate that kind of conflict?

Now, to put my cards on the table, I do have a particular philosophical anthropology. I don't have time to go into it, but I'll say this quickly. We are featherless, two-legged, linguistically conscious creatures born between urine and feces. That's a lot in common, isn't it? A whole lot in common. Our bodies will be the culinary delight of terrestrial worms one day. As the great Charles Darwin notes, we're vanishing creatures and disappearing organisms with language, on the way to death, on the way to extinction, at least in regard to our bodies.

What is significant about that? William James said it so well in the Gifford lectures: "Not the conception or the intellectual perception of evil, but the grisly blood-freezing heart-palsying sensation of it close upon one. . . . How irrelevantly remote seem all our usual refined optimisms and intellectual and moral consolations in presence of a need of help like this! Here is the real core of the religious problem: Help! Help!" That wonderful literary depiction of William James's Gifford lectures by Nathanael West—his real name was Nathan Weinstein; he renamed himself—in *Miss Lonelyhearts*, that first chapter: "Miss Lonelyhearts, Help Me, Help Me."

Relative impotence and relative failure, even given our Promethean efforts, haunt we human beings in science and religion. We use our empathy and imagination in science by predicting and controlling nature in the face of mystery. We use our empathy and imagination in religion by constructing structures of meaning and feeling in the face of death. George Santayana had it right in *Winds of Doctrine*. He said "Religion is the love of life in the consciousness of impotence."

That's worth coughing over (excuse my cold).

Our human "limit situations" the grand Karl Jaspers used to talk about are real—death, dread, disappointment. We know our English word *human* comes from the Latin *humando*, which means "burying." This "burying" signifies not only our finitude. It also reminds us of our limits and constraints, of what Plato called *Ananke* in the *Timaeus*, of what we run up against. Our radical finitude should accent our humble fallibility—in science and religion.

So you would think and hope that we can broaden the scope of empathy and imagination, both in the dialogue between secular brothers and sisters—atheistic, agnostic—and religious brothers and sisters. But most important for me is the prophetic twist, because I decided forty-nine years ago to pursue a calling—not just a career, a vocation, not just a profession. It was in Shiloh Baptist Church, a black church. We talked about Martin Luther King Jr., somebody who found unadulterated joy in loving and serving others, be they in chocolate cities, brown barrios, vanilla suburbs, or red reservations.

I was deeply impressed. I went to hear him speak. I was persuaded. Something was going on at the level of *paideia*. At the deepest level of soul, mind, body, and heart, something was going on in this young black boy in Sacramento, California. But it was prophetic. It was connected to that ninth thesis of the great Walter Benjamin that my dear sister Judith invoked earlier: History as catastrophe, the piling of wreckage on wreckage, the pile of debris, the wasted potential, the unrealized possibility of precious persons. We could begin by looking at the bottom of the Atlantic Ocean and seeing millions of African bodies there. But in nearly every ocean and land we see the same thing—cycles of domination, violence, bigotry, subordination, and hatred.

The prophetic twist—and here I follow the great Rabbi Abraham Joshua Heschel in his classic work, *The Prophets*—for the first time in human history we have a prophetic tradition. Yes, it was a Jewish invention—not that Jewish brothers and sisters follow through in practice, but it was a breakthrough of the Jewish folk in the past. All of us fall short of it. But there is a prophetic way of being in the world, a call for help, grounded in the cries of an oppressed people that warrants attention, and, in fact, to be human is to love the orphan, the widow, the stranger, to treat that non-Jewish other with dignity, with loving kindness.

This was a great breakthrough—an ethical revolution in the history of our species. In some ways even our secular moral discourses are just rich footnotes to it. OK, you don't have a cognitive commitment to God. Fine. I see you still love justice. Ah, Jacques Derrida, when he turned to ethics and politics, even he posited an a priori claim to justice all of a sudden. All of this deconstructive activity, calling everything into question, and lo and behold, you're still tied to the fifth chapter of Amos: "Let justice roll down like waters, and righteousness like a mighty stream"? Interesting, Jacques Derrida. We love you, God bless your soul.

I'm with him. He doesn't need to have a cognitive commitment to God, in that sense. But it's the prophetic, this sense of really believing, in the short time that we are here, that something called "Love thy neighbor," Leviticus 19:18, and justice being what love looks like in public in that tradition, even for the first-century Palestinian Jew named Jesus, who comes out of prophetic Judaism, is Jewish to the core. But Jesus has a logic, not only of equivalence—love thy neighbor—but also a logic of superabundance, to use the wonderful distinction of the late and great Paul Ricoeur. The logic of superabundance is what? Love thy enemy.

Oh, my God, Jesus has lost his mind.

What effects and consequences it generates in terms of keeping track of the catastrophic—that's what I want to know, just briefly. We'll save good time for dialogue.

The centrality of the catastrophic that sits at the center of prophetic religion, Shelley and Byron, prophetic poets—the catastrophic, the suffering of oppressed people, not in any kind of abstract way, not in any kind of condescending way, not in any kind of philanthropic or charitable way; justice being not just in solidarity with dominated peoples but of actually having a genuine love and willingness to celebrate with and work alongside those catching hell—with the wretched of the earth, in the language of Frantz Fanon.

How broad, how deep is your empathy? How broad, how deep is one's imagination? Right back to Shelley. And most importantly for me—and this is something that makes it difficult for a blues man like myself to remain for too long in an academic context—when you have that kind of orientation, you're always full of righteous indignation and holy anger at injustice. There's a sense of urgency, a state of emergency that has been normalized, hidden, and concealed. So you get a little suspicious sometimes of the discourses that can easily deodorize the funk that's there, that don't really want to engage the catastrophic, the way in which the U.S. Constitution didn't want to talk about the near-genocidal impact on our red brothers and sisters or the slavery of black people and act as if they don't exist.

We saw the same thing with Barack Obama in Philadelphia, with the race speech: "Slavery was America's original sin." No, no, no. You had already conquered and dominated indigenous peoples. They're both affairs of white supremacy, but one came first.

Don't deodorize that funk. Their lives are just as precious as any other human life on the globe, no matter what color, what culture, what civilization. We must attempt to always ensure that things are not so sterilized and sanitized. What I find so fascinating is that when we talk about the future of capitalist civilization—with the U.S. empire in decline and its culture in decay—and its democratic possibilities waning, can we imagine having a public discourse without there being voices—not just echoes, voices—keeping track of the catastrophic, so that unaccountable elites at the top don't run amok with greed and narrow empathy and truncated imagination?

We're right here in New York City. Wall Street is just right down the way, right? My God. Thank God for Paul Krugman. But the catastrophic conditions and circumstances right now, in light of corporate elites and financial oligarchs, with greed running amok, looting billions and billions of dollars, when 21 percent of America's children live in poverty—that's a crime against humanity. And people will say so 150 years from now. They'll look back and say, "What were they doing?" in the same way we look back at Thomas

Jefferson and say, "Oh, freedom and slavery." Very human, very hypocritical. But its true for all of us. True for all of us.

How do we create conditions under which the kind of tradition my dear sister Judith was talking about—remembrance and resistance, remembrance of suffering, not just the suffering of our own mothers and fathers, though they ought to be first.

I do believe in priorities. That's why I start with my mother. She's the ultimate Negro and my father is the coultimate Negro. I begin by loving Negroes first. I can't love anybody else if I don't love them, especially being shaped by people who were taught to hate themselves. That's another lecture.

But how do you then allow it to spill over so that there's a robust kind of poetic orientation, so that your empathy is so broad and your imagination is so open-ended that you're willing to be open to different discourses, arguments, pushing you against the wall. That's why many of my heroes tend to be atheistic and agnostic ones, like Chekhov—there's more empathy and imagination in Chekhov than 99 percent of Christian churches—or Beckett, a lapsed Christian who loves in the darkness; or Kafka, the catastrophic at the very beginning in *The Metamorphosis*—look at that unbelievable compassion flowing from Gregor to his violin-playing sister. My grand hero still breathing is Toni Morrison, who happens to be Catholic and black.

But dealing with the catastrophic and the response to the catastrophic—Ralph Waldo Ellison used to say, "The blues ain't nothing but an autobiographical chronicle of a personal catastrophe expressed lyrically." It's a lyrical response to catastrophe.

"Nobody loves me but my mama and she may be jivin', too." That's B. B. King, King of the Blues. Like Sophocles's sublime *Antigone*, catastrophe envelopes him, but unlike her his voice and song of empathy and imagination have the last word.

The strange fruit that southern trees bear—that's called American terrorism, lynching, almost ninety years. That's Billie Holiday, with Jewish brother Meeropol writing the lyrics ("Strange Fruit").

How do we deal with the catastrophic when we cast a light on it and have the courage to confront it and, most important, have the courage to organize and mobilize, to bring our voices together, in order to pressure those in power?

I'm going to close with the notion of "utopian interruptions." What I'm talking about is always tied to failure. It's no accident that the figures that I invoke—Beckett has an aesthetic for failure, doesn't he? So does Chekhov. So does Kafka. That wonderful letter that Benjamin writes to Gershom Scholem, July 1938: "You'll never understand the purity and the beauty of Kafka if you don't view him as a failure." Of course, if it wasn't for Max Brod, we wouldn't even have the text. Kafka believed he was a failure through and through.

Or, as Beckett says in his last piece of prose fiction *Worstword Ho*, "Try again. Fail again. Fail better."

Try again. Fail again. Fail better. Like Sheldon Wolin's fugitive democracy, prophetic religion is a fugitive affair—an empathetic and imaginative power that confronts hegemonic powers always operating. Prophetic religion is a profoundly tragicomic affair.

The dominant forms of religion are well-adjusted to greed and fear and bigotry. Hence well-adjusted to the indifference of the status quo toward poor and working people. Prophetic religion is an individual and collective performative praxis of maladjustment to greed, fear, and bigotry. For prophetic religion the condition of truth is to allow suffering to speak. Yet it is always tied to some failure—always. There are moments, like the 1960s in capitalist civilization or the 1980s in communist civilization that prophetic awaking takes place. It doesn't last too long, because the powers-that-be are not just mighty, but they're very clever and they dilute and incorporate in very seductive ways—or sometimes they just kill you!

In this age of Obama many of us broke our necks to bring the age of Reagan and the era of conservatism to a close. Now, with the age of Obama, the question becomes: Can prophetic religion, in all of its various forms, mobilize people, generate levels of righteous indignation against injustice—not raw rage at persons, not ad hominem attacks—can we put pressure on President Obama? He's listening to technocratic elites in his economic team who have never had any serious concern with poor people and working people. He's mesmerized by their braininess and seduced by their establishment status and Wall Street connections. The same is true with his neoimperial team in foreign policy. President Obama's charismatic version of American exceptionalism promotes Keynesian neoliberalism at home and liberal neoconservatism abroad. This is confusing to some, but clear to prophetic religious and secular folk who love poor and working people.

But what's fascinating is, he was able to mobilize based on a democratic rhetoric and ended up with technocratic policies. We've seen that before. He's got progressive instincts. Will he stand up? We won't even talk about healthcare. My God.

But, in talking about prophetic religion, we're talking about something that is engaging, something that is risk taking, and it has everything to do with the enabling virtue, which is courage—the courage to expand empathy, expand imagination, think critically, organize, mobilize, and maybe, like Brother Martin Luther King Jr., pay the ultimate price. But it's all in bearing witness. Bearing witness, that's what the call is about. That's what the vocation is about.

And I'm so glad I could bear witness a little bit here. Thank you so much.

DIALOGUE

Judith Butler and Cornel West

EDUARDO MENDIETA: Judith, this situation, the exilic situation or condition, can we translate that into an ethics for a U.S. citizen? How would we translate that into an ethics of citizenship in our present context? Or is it only applicable to Jews?

JUDITH BUTLER: Eduardo, I guess I want to say that I think we have to start with the distinction between the citizen and the noncitizen, because we also have a politics which involves refusing to grant citizenship to a vast domain of the population, who, nevertheless, work here, constitute who we are, who we might even say have become indigenous or have acquired indigenous status, because they are not entitled and not enfranchised.

I worry very much about using citizenship as the framework without actually thinking about how that distinction between citizen and noncitizen is also imposed here. I worry that a lot of our own notions of pluralism and even our ideas about communitarianism assume already enfranchised communities or already visible communities. But how do those communities actually get constituted through the production and erasure of nonpublic and disenfranchised communities?

So it's that relationship that I would like to think about. What breaks through? What are the moments in which the population without working papers or the population without citizenship nevertheless appears? I think the singing of the national anthem in public in Los Angeles by a number of undocumented workers was a kind of astonishing moment, where the anthem was sung in Spanish and in English both.

But I think there are other ways in which the amnesiac surface of our everyday politics has to be broken so that we actually see who the workers are on whom we depend and to whom we extend no rights, who are the populations that are living here fearful of getting ill because there is no possibility of health insurance and there is no clear guarantee that they will even be accepted into hospitals.

So perhaps we have our own dispossessed and we are haunted by the dispossessed, or we fail to be haunted by the dispossessed, and we need to think about what an ethics would be that would help us rethink the relationship between the citizen and the noncitizen now.

MENDIETA: One more question, in terms of this ethics of memory—won't that make us, perhaps, overly nostalgic, always looking backward? Then we might lose sight of how to gauge progress. How do we start thinking about progress if we are always thinking from the standpoint of an ethics of memory, of memorialization?

BUTLER: I think it's not so much an ethics of memory or memorialization. Maybe "remembrance" in Benjamin's terms is a little different. It's not that we turn to the past and lose ourselves in the past. It's rather that the past flashes up in what he calls "the time of the now," the *Jetztzeit*. What actually happens is that something about our present experience is interrupted by what he calls an image of the past, but I think we could translate that in several different ways. Some undocumented or unarchived history of oppression emerges within our contemporary life and makes us rethink the histories we have told about how we got from one place in history to the present.

It also, I think, has the effect of producing converging temporalities in the present, which allows us to reorient ourselves in nonidentitarian ways so that we are not just looking out for our own history or our own people, but our history turns out to be interrupted fundamentally by an effaced history. I think Cornel's example of the effacement of the genocide against native peoples in this country is exactly such a moment. Do we allow that amnesia to continue? What are the public moments in which that amnesia is broken apart?

I think it not only recalls us to a past—or, rather, lets the past into the present—but it reorients us toward a broader, more capacious idea of social justice.

So I'm not sure about progress. I guess I'm maybe too much with Benjamin and Kafka in this way.

CORNEL WEST: And you juxtapose the last line of Adorno's great essay on progress, where he defined progress as resistance against the mainstream, where the alternative is capitulation—you juxtapose that line with the first line from Marcuse's *Eros and Civilization*: "All Utopian thought is predicated on some memory of plenitude."

That's Marcuse's romantic tie to Schiller. Adorno is much more dialectically dark, closer to Kafka.

But it's a fascinating tension. Adorno, like Benjamin, is calling into question a dominant notion of progress. For them this notion of progress constitutes catastrophe, and the best we do—the dialectic is at a standstill—is put our foot on the brake to stop the dominating elite from just looting everything. That's what the Obama lecture was about. He was weakly gesturing at just putting the brakes on the capitalist civilization gone mad—short-term thinking, ecological crisis, climate warming, and so forth. But his democratic rhetoric was only symbolic: the substance lies in his technocratic policies. Here comes Obama with charisma, wonderful rhetoric. He looks pleasant. We know if he looked like the late, great Isaac Hayes, he would not have won that election.

But we love our brother. We love our brother. He is just the friendly face of the U.S. empire in relative decline.

But you have to put the brake on. And that can only be done by empathic and imaginative citizens organized and mobilized for deep democratic ends and aims. That's part of utopian interruption. Stop the madness that is oftentimes at work when it comes to the treatment of poor and working people.

BUTLER: I think moving forward has to be distinguished from progress. One reason that progress is linked to catastrophe is that it produces debris that it cannot assimilate into its own narrative structure, so that debris keeps on piling up. What cannot be brought forward? What is left behind? There's always something left behind, especially in aggressive notions of progress that hold out the promise of a kind of final redemption.

MENDIETA: I'm thinking along the lines of the question—we are linking progress to secularization, which is an instance of modernization. The question was also a way to ask you, how do we uncouple modernizing progress from secularization? You have demonstrated how we have all of these incredible resources in very Jewish philosophers. If we're going to move forward, we would have to give up that.

BUTLER: I do worry that some of the conceptual frameworks we have for linking secularization with modernization actually assume certain kinds of religions as the relevant ones. Which religion got secularized? Which set of religions is left behind, which now, as Thomas Friedman would say about Islam, represent the premodern?

So I'm not sure secularization has brought all religions with it. We might actually think a little bit about whether there is a kind of presumptive Christian presupposition there and whether it's also a Christianity that is, in some sense, divided from Judaism—

which is, of course, not what Cornel does—and whether all of the other religions that have remained unspeakable here today even count as part of that story.

I guess I'm way back there. I haven't arrived yet in this narrative.

WEST: I think there are two senses of secularization that are important.

One, I think it's very important to acknowledge the moral and political breakthrough of liberalism against the kings, because when you provide that space for rights and liberties across the board, especially if it's broad in its empathy and imagination—all-inclusive in that sense—that is a grand historic breakthrough, though it remains fragile and fleeting.

At the same time, it's clear that the Weberian thesis about disenchantment of the world—resulting in fewer cognitive commitments to God-talk—is not true. It was never true in the United States, but it's certainly not true around the world now. So we have to hold onto the liberal political, moral breakthrough and try to make the breakthrough on the economic level in terms of democratizing, but also acknowledge that Durkheim was actually more right than Weber, in *The Elementary Forms of Religious Life*. Think about page 431. He says there's something eternal about worship and faith. And if you shift from God-talk, you could end up worshipping the market or its accompaniments and accoutrements. You can end up with idolatrous worship of a lot of profane things. It reminds one of Joseph Conrad's *Heart of Darkness*.

You are going to treasure something. What is it? Is it Kurtz and the ivory? That's Conrad, 1899, the critique of idolatry. Christians like myself say you must forever be vigilant in critiques of idolatry. Why? Because idolatry is shot through all of us.

But you're going to treasure something. If you treasure something that pulls you out of yourself and makes you love more and sacrifice for justice, that's going to be better than the next Lexus that you get. There's no escape from the fiduciary dimension of being human.

BUTLER: May I ask Cornel a question? Cornel, talk to us about treasuring something, valuing something, and worshipping something. Are they interchangeable in your vocabulary?

WEST: I would just say "treasure." Let's just say "treasure."

BUTLER: Let's just say "treasure"?

WEST: Yes.

BUTLER: You're stepping back.

WEST: In your mind, what's the difference?

BUTLER: I don't know. It's interesting. On the one hand, you talk about worshipping, and you talk about being vigilant against idolatry. For many people, worshipping is idolatry. You are actually offering us a distinction. I was just making an opening for you.

WEST: I've got to decide whether to walk through that opening or not.

MENDIETA: Here's another question while you think on that one. This is a question inspired by Jürgen Habermas's work. Don't you think that perhaps our state hasn't been secularized enough? This is from the other side. You called us to accept and understand the plurality of religious beliefs. But there's one thing that brings a knot to my throat, and that's when the president always has to invoke, "God bless America," as though we are ordering God.

On the other side, as a prophetic citizen, how do you feel about that, when the president invokes this God?

WEST: I don't like it. I do not like it. It's like Pilate saying, "Jesus, I really do like you, but you've got to go." There is a line there. But it's part of the rhetoric of the thing.

But I don't take it that seriously. It's like, every January, the president says, "There is no problem we cannot solve because we are Americans." That's just the religion of possibility. It's part of

American self-understanding. It's a lie. There are problems Americans cannot solve.

But it's that sense of strenuous mood-generating energy and so forth.

I would say this, though, in regard to the point you made to Professor Habermas. Secularization is one thing. For me, the priority is a democratization of the state, which has to do with the substantive accountability and answerability of corporate elites and financial oligarchs who are running amok in terms of might, status, and reshaping the nation, and much of the world, in their image. That's very dangerous. It is very dangerous. It is as dangerous as kings and queens running amok in the seventeenth and eighteenth centuries—unaccountable elites. The history of democracies is the awakening of the demos who try to impose some kinds of regulations, some kinds of controls on them for the public good. It's clear that, for the most part, elites have the public interest and the common good as an afterthought in their market calculations.

MENDIETA: When you talked about utopian interruptions, I was thinking immediately of Ernst Bloch, not just *The Principle of Hope*, but also and especially of his book *Atheism in Christianity*. There he begins by saying that the true Christian must be atheist, and the atheist is the Christian.

This is a relationship to antifetishism, anti-idolatry; and, while remaining profoundly Christian, how do we live up to that challenge of Bloch?

WEST: I think we have to live that tension. We have to live that tension. By living that tension, what that means is that we are forever aspiring and then falling short, but calling into question the ways in which we become deferential to idols or the ways in which we become not empathetic enough, not imaginative enough, not courageous enough, and so on.

But I think that that kind of creative tension is part and parcel of what it is, partly, just to be human, in terms of having ideals that fall short in their realization. OK, you don't want to engage in God-talk. There's always the gap between your ideals and what is real. That gap is where you have to live. There's going to be a tension. Of course, for religious persons, it's tied to not just God but all the various stories that try to keep us honest and keep us candid about how we're falling short and when we're making some breakthroughs.

But that's another reason why certain revolutionary moments—it could be Alain Badiou's 1968 in Paris and the event that means so much to him, it could be the movement led by Martin Luther King Jr. or it could be the Stonewall rebellion or it could be the populist movement in the 1890s—these moments in which this unbelievable courage of fellow human beings emerged and they were willing to put everything on the line—I would say, even in relation to the struggle against fascism. I'm in solidarity with Churchill. That's a rare thing for me. He's fighting fascism. He believes black people are subhuman, supports colonialism in India and Africa, but he's fighting Hitler. I'm in his army, because I'm fighting Hitler, too. I just got some other white-supremacist matters to attend to once the war is over.

Does that make sense?

MENDIETA: Absolutely, absolutely.

BUTLER: It's interesting, because it's the reverse of loving your own people first. You have to love your own people first, but sometimes the political principles—you have to put other people first and then you have to come back to your own. Interesting.

WEST: That's true. That's a wonderful way of putting it.

CONCLUDING DISCUSSION

Judith Butler, Jürgen Habermas,
Charles Taylor, Cornel West

CRAIG CALHOUN: I want to just set up the occasion for all four of our speakers to speak with each other briefly at the end. I'm going to do it by trying to give you a gloss on what they said so that they can speak to each other about how I got it wrong.

One of the things that we heard here was that secularity isn't just a religion problem. It's not even just a political institution. Secularity, secularism, the problem with the secular, has to do with inhabiting a common world without universally shared absolutes or notions of the transcendence of that worldliness. It's a problem that is set up by being in that predicament together, with history, which is both the weight of the past history and the openness to the future—a product, as Cornel told us, of power and catastrophe, not only progress. That creates the occasion for politics, in the sense of making a world in common, at least making social institutions parts of this world that make it common, in an Arendtian sense, always in relation to historically given diversity and connections, both sides of that, including competing claims to and refusals of the universal.

The predicament is the one of diversity that Judith told us about, and that diversity includes people who want to not recognize the diversity and assert the universal in one way or another. There are issues of power and exclusion that structure this on religious and nonreligious grounds.

Then we have the question of solidarity, the establishment of mutual belonging. This includes but, as Judith just said, isn't limited to citizenship. It's structured by the very limitations of citizenship.

In that context, we have questions that both Jürgen and Chuck took up about the capacity to share a discursive world, to share common beliefs, and to make that the basis for creating institutions and solving problems through the state. Discursive mediation in democracy and republican forms of government come to the fore here. Jürgen talked about the attempt to abstract from that which could not be shared and to find a way to stay in the realm of what could be shared, bracketing the language and other problems that limit sharing, and relying on discourse ethics.

Charles Taylor talked about a recognition, as he would say, of a kind of incommensurability of various sorts and limits that are not unique to religion but cut across a variety of kinds of difference, and also about practices of recognition and inclusion and self-restraint in the face of that incommensurability.

Judith Butler talked about protections for alterity in this context as being also basic and as being something that is not grasped entirely in the discursive mediation, the establishment of the commonality there, the sharing; a recognition of and obligations to suffering, not to identity, and the exilic situation shaping this; an idea of justice in the face of power and violence, which, if I hear rightly, is put forward as also a basis for commonality, just like that discursive construction of common beliefs or practices might be, and comes sometimes from religious sources or traditions.

Cornel called to our attention another dimension, the creation of empathy—if you will, the poetry and art and music of religion, including religion—and prophecy in response to domination, discord, and disaster—keeping track of catastrophe, as he put it—and, I would add, overcoming blindness, making yourself see, finding the resources to see what you are missing, which is also not the process of simply achieving a shared set of beliefs or solving various problems in the state. He suggested that this is a problem in religion, as it is elsewhere.

We had a discourse about the way to achieve a shared basis for politics and common beliefs, a discourse rooted in the limit of that possibility for commonality, first with Charles Taylor talking about the incompletely shareable, the incommensurabilities among a wide variety of positions, and then with Judith Butler talking about starting from alterity and diversity. We had a discussion of the centrality of empathy, that this isn't going to happen in rational discourse alone, if it's going to happen at all. I think Cornel stressed that.

Did I get it partly right, at least? Charles?

CHARLES TAYLOR: I think you got it so right that we should now step to the next phase.

I think there is a very important theme that has emerged from all four of us which is worth looking at, which goes beyond the question of the static way in which religion and nonreligion coexist and looks at the way in which these very deep insights can leap over the boundaries from religious to nonreligious or from nonreligious to religious.

Jürgen has taken this up under the rubric of the translation of certain religious ideas into secular reason. I see it in Judith and also in Cornel. Let me give the example I like to look at, which is very important here, this Arendtian idea that we don't choose the people we share the world with. The idea of choosing is deeply wrong.

Here you get something which is a very profound theological, Jewish and Christian, idea: The world is a gift. We are given to each other. We can't choose. This is part of what we are, this gift.

You then can take it outside the gift, to some degree, and translate it outside that theological idea of the gift. This again connects up with the prophetic. What do we think of this process? This, I think, is a very interesting question, which we may get different opinions on. Does this process end at a certain point? Do you sort of exhaust the ideas of the other side and then you have kind of translated it into your own world and you forget the source? Or is there something, in principle, endless, inexhaustible, about this kind of exchange—which is, interestingly, the positive side, of which the negative side is fights for secularization against religion or religion against secularization?

Another example, of course, is the Truth and Reconciliation Commission in South Africa, which is definitely a Christian idea of forgiveness, which then got retranslated and put in another context.

In other words, thinking of how we're going to coexist as religious and nonreligious people, are we going to make the translations and then just forget about each other; or is this a potentially inexhaustible process, which I think it is? That's something worth looking at.

JUDITH BUTLER: I'm glad that you brought up the question of translation, because it seems to me something that the two of you—you both used the term *translation,* but I didn't actually hear any reflection on what translation means or what actually happens when a translation takes place.

Of course, because I'm working on Benjamin, I'm very aware that translation is a very complex kind of process. It seemed to me that the way it was being used is that, when a religious claim is translated into secular reason, the religious part is somehow left behind and the translation is an extraction of the truly rational element from the religious formulation, and we do leave the religious behind as so much dross.

I'm not sure translation ever works that way. I wonder whether the residues of the theological continue to resonate within what we understand as the secular. I think this is really important. I also think there are accounts of universality—which was one of the things I was trying to explore—accounts of universality, of equality, and, say, of cohabitation that emerge from within religious discourse. I'm not sure that they can be fully extracted from it.

Myself, I'm not so much interested in the common, which I think is what Craig—I think maybe it's the uncommon, or what is not part of the common or what can never truly become common, which establishes really specific differences, and which also becomes the basis of an ethical relation that establishes alterity rather than the common as the basis of ethicality. I think we can't have an empathy, we can't have the relation to the suffering of others without that constitutive difference.

I think those are two points I wanted to make.

One last small point. It seemed to me that Jürgen Habermas was saying that religious motivations are one thing, but legitimation must have a rational form that is distinct from whatever religious motivation leads us to the insight into that reason—

CALHOUN: Justification.

BUTLER: Yes. It seems to me that Charles Taylor was actually saying there can be religious modes of valuation which have to finally submit to a neutral state. I think that those modes of valuation, which include justificatory schemes, also translate into the "neutral" state.

I'm wondering about what makes any of us think that translations are successful, whether translation can and does succeed. I'm wondering whether it can and does succeed.

CALHOUN: If I understand—this is a question for Jürgen and Chuck—from a position not assuming commonality but suggesting that alterity may be the more fundamental condition and the more ethically central condition—

BUTLER: That was for you (Calhoun)

PROF. CALHOUN: That's what I thought you said in your talk, and what I thought I summarized was the talk. That then raises the stakes of this idea that translation might establish commonality, if it's bridging this sort of serious alterity.

So the question to each of you is, do you think translation can work in a strong sense?

BUTLER: And if so, how?

JÜRGEN HABERMAS: I will come back to translation, but let me first express that I feel that I am in a double bind after listening to Cornel West. Only a few hundred meters up from Wall Street here, we hear not someone talking about prophetic speech, but performing it in some way—namely, in a kind of moving rhetoric to which the only possible response would be to stand up and to change one's life. So just to continue academic discourse is somehow ridiculous.

The other side of the double bind is that we are here in an institution and following a format.

So let me come back to the issue of translation. Of course, there is a misapplication of what we usually mean by translation, even if the two of us don't mean the same thing. What I have in mind is the task of translating not from a religious discourse but from presentations in a religious language to a public language, which allows us to arrive at reasons that are more general than the ones in the original language. This wider accessibility and appeal of reasons is the idea I connect with "the secular," reasons which are secular in the sense of transcending the semantic domains of particular religious communities, that reach even beyond the generalizing move that was originally connected with the term *secularization,* from within the Christian Church anyway.

Here in the United States even my closest philosophical friends confront me often with the fact that any discourse leads to disagreements if you push the argument only one step further than the apparent agreement. They present a picture of language and communication as a medium that produces differences. Of course, I am the last to deny the fact of pluralism and the host of corresponding reasonable disagreements. But I would rather explain them in sociological terms of growing social complexity and functional differentiation, etc.

I think that communication works under the opposite pressure of reaching agreements, at least when it comes to politics. If it comes to politics, this is like everyday face-to-face interaction. In both cases we are moving in a rather thick context, at least in a context where we cannot but cooperate, whether we like it or not, whether we just are in the kitchen and cooperate in making a meal or whether we have to find a way, for example, in this country, to establish a public option in the health care reform bill. There is a pressure for cooperation that we cannot escape.

Given this situation, I find, like Rawls, the Kantian term of the *public use of reason* in the political public sphere appealing—it serves as one way of explaining certain ethical expectations of citizenship.

In this muddy, informal communication network of the public sphere, there is upon the minds of citizens a pressure to make contributions to a democratic process which is designed to reach, finally, a decision for collectively binding programs. Under this constraint, I think that, specifically, the interaction of religious and nonreligious citizens could evoke repressed, forgotten, unused intuitions that are somewhere buried. The interaction can work both ways. In the best of cases, the rationalizing force of one side meets the powerful images of a world-disclosing language on the other side.

Call it a mutual evocation of something that can only be said in their own language. But in this communication some people's languages are more open, and their reasons more accessible and appealing to wider circles than other people's. If all goes well, the outcome is not disagreement, nor is it strict translation either, but lifting for wider public semantic potentials what would otherwise remain sunken in the idiom of particular religious communities.

CALHOUN: Cornel, can you be tempted into this conversation?

CORNEL WEST: It looks like the point had to do with the scope of generalization, right?

HABERMAS: Yes.

WEST: It strikes me as plausible, absolutely. I don't have anything to add in regard to that.

TAYLOR: I would like to answer Judith's question. I don't think *translation* is the best word—I just used it because I wanted to refer to Jürgen—except the older meaning of *translation*. When you talked about a bishop moving from one diocese to another, it was also called *translation*. But it's a jumping over the boundary. And, of course, something is left behind. It's a different kind of context for the meaning.

But the interesting phenomenon is that when these insights jump over these boundaries and inspire people, and then they find, maybe, another language for it—and you're quite right, very often the original spark is still burning there. If this is another dimension to existing indifference, different from the sort of static one of how we're going to work it out so we don't fight and make these ground rules, different from, "we're all stuck in our positions and we don't want to look too closely at the other one, but we're going to somehow not fight." It's quite different—it is some kind of real creative, inspiring move, which I think can very often bring everybody farther ahead.

That is one of the aspects of this, the nonidentical, where the whole idea of leveling it down to—"clearly, all the terms for public discourse are going to be forever because we've got it neutralized between them all"—is the very, very wrong view. There is this phenomenon. It's very interesting to study it. Gandhi is another example. You read *Hind Swaraj* and, in some ways, you're totally shocked, because it is so antimodern, so anti-industrialization, so antidevelopment. But there's working up there a fantastic vision of nonviolent resistance and what it can produce. It jumps over to Martin Luther King and it jumps over to Manila. This is fantastic. It comes from a mixed context of Hindu thought and certain Christian inspiration, and then it jumps over all these fences.

That is, I think, the most valuable phenomenon in our life of diversity. Just thinking of it as a problem that we have to find neutral language for is wrong—it's a curmudgeon attitude that we don't need.

CALHOUN: This has been an extraordinary discussion. Thank you all.

AFTERWORD: RELIGION'S MANY POWERS

CRAIG CALHOUN

Religion is threatening, inspiring, consoling, provocative, a matter of reassuring routine or calls to put one's life on the line. It is a way to make peace and a reason to make war. As the great Iranian sociologist and Islamic reformer Ali Sharyati put it: "Religion is an amazing phenomenon that plays contradictory roles in peoples lives. It can destroy or revitalize, put to sleep or awaken, enslave or emancipate, teach docility or teach revolt."[1] No wonder debates about religion in the public sphere can be so confusing.

The prominence of religion still has the capacity to startle secular thinkers who thought it was clearly destined to fade in the face of enlightenment and modernity. Jürgen Habermas, the most prominent social and political theorist of our age, may have been among the startled. Certainly he startled others when, after decades of analyzing the public sphere in entirely secular terms, he insisted that religion needed central attention.

Though they seem new to some, these issues appear to us now in a perspective that has been forming since the 1970s. It is shaped by the rise of Evangelical Christianity and the prominence of the "new religious right" in the U.S. It is sharpened by Western anxiety about Islam, which is old but made current by the conflict over Palestine and Israel, armed confrontations that have been nearly continuous since the Yom Kippur War and extend into terrorist tactics deployed in the West, the OPEC crisis and awareness of growing Arab wealth, the Iranian Revolution, and the immigration of Muslims to Europe. The prominence of Ultra-Orthodox Jews unsettles Israeli politics (and that of some American municipalities). The sense that religion matters more in public is reinforced by growth of both Islam and Christianity around the world, including in the former Soviet Union and East Asian countries. The sense that it is poorly understood is informed by new conservative alliances that unsettle the Anglican communion, link African bishops to American parishes, and make a special issue of homosexuality. Hispanic migrants to the US have not only changed American Catholicism but also in large numbers joined Pentecostal and Evangelical churches—a trend also present, if less pronounced, in Central and South America.

But confusion and struggles over religion in the public sphere are much older than this. Religion has been a source of anxiety for the liberal public sphere at least since the English Civil War. Debate then was intense. It was conducted both in print and in public meetings. It connected members of different classes, different regions of the country. It mobilized the greatest thinkers of the day and it mobilized people who hadn't learned to read. It addressed the most basic questions of the nature of English society and the extent to which citizens could choose the institutions and moral order under which they would live. It also addressed the most basic questions of astronomy and physics, the nature of science, and the possibility that new knowledge could transform the world. And indeed, it addressed the most basic questions of religion, the relation of human beings to God, whether and how God intervened in the temporal world, and how religious authority should relate to politics. The seventeenth-century English debates helped to create what we now call the modern world as well as the idea of public reason as a central part of that world. They also led to regicide and civil war. The emerging theory of a reasoned public sphere was partly a response to religiously informed conflicts. These left many of the best thinkers of the next century profoundly afraid of zealotry and fanaticism. Much thinking about the public sphere was devoted not simply to ensuring openness but to disciplining participants so that conviction would not eliminate the capacity to entertain contrary views and faith would not become "enthusiasm"—the determination to act immediately on inspiration without the mediation of reflection or reason.

These issues informed the founding of the United States, and American history reminds us how recurrently central they are. Protection of religious freedom was a central theme in debates shaping both federal and state constitutions. Protection of those professing a non-Christian faith, or no religious faith at all, was bundled with concern that the new government should not favor one among several versions of Christianity active in the colonies. Each might present a "comprehensive worldview," but both the constitution and public understanding recognized the legitimacy of a plurality of such worldviews. The idea of an institutionalized separation of church and state was discussed, but, as Charles Taylor notes, only gained momentum much later. Christian values and rhetoric were central to the public life of the country. Indeed, the single greatest conflict in the history of the American republic was understood in profoundly religious, and specifically Christian, terms. These were the terms of battlefield prayers but also political justifications. While Southerners reached back to Aristotle for doctrines of natural slavery, they also relied on the Bible to justify a form of domination most Christians now consider beyond the pale. But, if there was a religious movement that changed the course of American history by its interventions in the public sphere, it was the anti-slavery movement. From eighteenth-century Wesleyan and Moravian opposition to the slave trade to the conviction that slavery was a "national sin" that spread during the Second Great Awakening, the opposition to slavery was in large part a Christian intervention in the public sphere.[2]

The Social Gospel movement of the later nineteenth and early twentieth centuries addressed social issues from inequality and slums to crime and the need for better schools. It stretched into pacifist opposition to World War I. It informed the development of settlement houses and ministry to immigrants and the poor—and even early social science (though, for some, social science was a secular channeling of initially religious impulses). As Walter Rauschenbusch, one of the leading preachers of the Social Gospel, argued: "Whoever uncouples the religious and the social life has not understood Jesus. Whoever sets any bounds for the reconstructive power of the religious life over the social relations and institutions of men, to that extent denies the faith of the Master."[3]

Religion was entangled in complicated ways with politics, trade unionism, and social activism during the early decades of the twentieth century—and not consistently on one side or the other. Christianity figured prominently in the populism of William Jennings Bryan and his followers. If Bryan's attacks on Darwinian evolutionary theory presaged one enduring theme engaging American Evangelicals in the public sphere, his populist attacks on bankers and others in Northeastern monied classes presaged another (and should remind us that religion is not inherently of the left or right). When Bryan thundered, "you shall not crucify mankind on a cross of gold," his target was a deflationary currency reform that threatened indebted farmers and other borrowers. But the power of the speech came significantly from its biblical allusions. Like many populists, Bryan was a complicated figure pressing issues from economic nationalism to prohibition, but always in solidarity with common people who benefited less than elites from the Gilded Age boom and suffered more after it went bust. Writing in 1922, John Dewey grasped that to many in the educated elite Bryan seemed at best backward, and his followers more so. Dewey noted that part of the issue was the place of religion in the public sphere. Bryan speaks, he said, for "the churchgoing classes, those who have come under the influence of evangelical Christianity." Yet, Dewey suggested, sophisticated elites ignored the populists at their peril. "These people form the backbone of phil-anthropic social interest, of social reform through political action, of pacifism, of popular education."[4] To be clear, Dewey—a "secular humanist"—was not endorsing Christianity or any other religion; he was criticizing elite condescension.

Churchgoing classes again figured centrally in the civil rights movement of the 1950s and '60s. Black churches were central to the mobilization, providing it with "free spaces" to organize, a network infrastructure, the Exodus narrative of liberation, much of its rheto-ric and many of its most important leaders including Dr. Martin Luther King Jr. Predominantly white churches contributed support, and proportionately Jewish support was even more important. The same goes for broader struggles against poverty and inequality (and as Jürgen Habermas notes, religiously framed concerns informed the young John Rawls as he began his lifelong focus on issues of jus-tice).[5] Opposition to the Vietnam War also drew on religious roots.

None of these mobilizations was specifically a religious movement. There was religious opposition to each. Yet each movement drew importantly on religious sources. These included not only motivations but also social networks, practical experience in public speaking, resources of physical space and funds, ideals of justice, visions of peace, language for grasping the connection between contemporary problems and deeper moral values, and capacities to both generate and recognize the power of prophetic disruptions to the complacency of everyday life. And if I have recounted these movements as an American story, that should not obscure the importance either of religiously informed internationalism from Christian participants in the Peace Corps or later humanitarian and human rights movements or the broader international context in which the American events were entwined with the rise of liberation theology in Latin America, the reforms of Vatican II, or the commitment to peace in the mainly Protestant ecumenical movement.

Yet, from the Social Gospel to the peace movement of the 1960s, there was also questioning about how much religion should inform the public sphere. There were many who advocated keeping religion within the private realm, perhaps influencing public action by giving it moral motivation or restricting it by shaping individual consciences. At the same time, many of public movements and institutions shed their religious identifications. The place of religious rhetoric in organizing public discourse declined (albeit unevenly, with mainline Protestants losing their voices faster than Catholics, and churches remaining more important in the black public sphere—alongside the Nation of Islam). Many, especially elites, understood this as simply part of a long-term, modernizing process of secularization. Accordingly, they paid too little attention to renewals of faith that gathered strength. Some of these, like Pentecostal Christianity, were minimally engaged in public life. There was a renewal of religious observance among Jews (shaped both by rising numbers of Orthodox, including Hasidim, and by revitalization of ritual participation among Reform and Conservative Jews). For the most part this was also "private," though Jewish public support for Israel, if anything, grew stronger after the Yom Kippur War (during which many Jews who had thought themselves simply secular were surprised by the extent of their own identification). And immigrants—various Asians, Hispanics, Russians, Arabs; Evangelicals, Orthodox Jews, Catholics, Buddhists, Muslims—also increased active religious participation rates with long-term implications for American religion, though initially without much public engagement.

But there was growing public engagement, mostly among what was quickly dubbed the "new religious right." Disproportionately Evangelical Christian, this movement built historically unprecedented bridges to Catholics, largely through participation in the anti-abortion movement, and also connections to some conservative Jews. These interdenominational connections eventually underwrote generic reference to "people of faith," but this shouldn't obscure the fact that for most, faith was specific not generic. Political alliances didn't mean ecumenical transformations of beliefs or rituals; demanding recognition as part of a widespread renewal of faith that included Muslims as well as Christians around the world—and to some extent Buddhists mobilized in new collective forms like Nichiren Shoshu or Tsu Chi—didn't mean that being religious became a substitute for being Muslim, Christian, Jewish, or Buddhist.

Most of America's educated elite, including social scientists, did not immediately recognize this as a challenge to the widespread "subtraction story" of secularization as simply the progressive removal of religion from the public sphere and eventually from more and more of life.[6] It was viewed more as an aberration than a trend or a continuation of a long-term pattern of ebb and flow in public religion. It was often analyzed with reference to the history of conservatism and rightist politics rather than to the history of public religion or for that matter populism. Part of Dewey's message in 1922 was that sophisticated elites (or those who understood themselves as such) failed to see the importance of populism because they looked down their noses at it. This remains true today, when the mobilizing frame is the Tea Party rather than the Moral Majority or Father Coughlin's American version of fascism. Neither populism nor religion (nor more specifically Evangelical Christianity) is inherently right wing or left. Populist anger and sense of disrespect and disenfranchisement can be appropriated and steered by rightist demagogues but also by more progressive social movements. Religiously informed criticism of existing social conditions—or moral outrage at specific abuses—can be voiced without allegiance to any specific political party or movement of the right or left, or it can be claimed with varying degrees of success for one brand of this-worldly, secular politics.

It has now been twenty-five years since Richard John Neuhaus wrote *The Naked Public Square*—an effort to understand what lay behind renewed religious mobilization on the right.[7] Neuhaus did not think the public square was actually "naked"; in fact he thought this an impossibility, for there could be no such thing as engaged democratic public life that didn't depend on and connect to citizens' deeper moral commitments. In the U.S., he argued, public life would necessarily involve religiously motivated and religiously framed participation, because a democratic public sphere was necessarily open to all citizens and open to them in terms they themselves had a central role in defining—and, in America, religion was important to most citizens. But, Neuhaus suggested, when so many believe in a public sphere stripped of religion, they actually, ironically, cede much of the democratic impulse in the public sphere to groups like the then prominent Moral Majority of the Rev. Jerry Falwell. The peril in this is not simply that the Moral Majority is conservative. It is that "it wants to enter the political arena making public claims on the basis of private truths." As Neuhaus continues: "The integrity of politics itself requires that such a proposal be resisted. Public decisions must be made by arguments that are public in character."[8] This is precisely the issue taken up in the present volume, most directly in Jürgen Habermas's opening contribution.

Neuhaus's argument was a call from a conservative but centrist position in American politics to recognize the power of religion in the public sphere. Such calls came earlier in the United States. But even in Europe—where religious practice declined most and secularization theory seemed most to apply—the issue of public religion is now very much on the agenda, partly because of anxiety over migration and Islam. It is often framed as contestation over the heritage of the Enlightenment. Many misleadingly assume the Enlightenment was essentially secular. And certainly there was a largely secular branch of eighteenth-century philosophy that had huge historical influence, not least when amplified by the anticlericalism spawned in France by the alliance of the Catholic Church to antirepublican reactionary politics. But the Enlightenment was also a movement among religious thinkers.[9] Joachim Israel calls this the "moderate" Enlightenment. The term is apt (though not Israel's implication that the "radical" Enlightenment was simply a more extreme and thereby purer, less compromised version of the same thing).[10] The project of religiously informed public reason was understood to depend on a certain moderation not of faith but of *enthusiasm*. This was the term—along with *fanatic*—used to describe Puritans and others in seventeenth-century England who insisted with absolute confidence on what was revealed by their "inner lights" and brooked no public compromises. The ideas of the enthusiasts as well as religious moderates and both monarchists and antimonarchists all circulated in a vibrant public sphere made possible by a combination of preaching and other oral performances and printed circulation of sermons, pamphlets, and other texts.[11]

Those who developed the idea that the public sphere was central to modern, especially democratic, society often described their own work as enlightenment—advancing the intellectual maturation of humanity—and in these terms they embraced resistance to enthusiasm. Emphases on education, discipline, and orderly conduct of public debates shaped elite views of how the public sphere should advance. Sometimes these became matters of class distinction; liberal elites feared the debasement of public life if nonelites were admitted.[12] The inclusive ideal of publicness has recurrently confronted arguments that exclusion was in fact necessary. Some of these have centered on religion. But, equally, religious thinkers have often held that public reason is not only an arbiter of policy decisions but also a vital means for advancing all sorts of understanding, even of religious convictions and their implications. Religious voices have remained active in the modern public sphere, sometimes in pursuit of enlightenment and sometimes in reaction to the Enlightenment or post-Enlightenment secularism. Even in Europe, secularization of public political debate only became pronounced after World War II.

Nonetheless, in both academic and public understanding, both the Enlightenment and the birth of the modern public sphere came to be understood in overwhelmingly secular terms. Jürgen Habermas's classic book, to which we owe today's commonplace usage of the term *public sphere,* is an influential case in point.[13] Habermas offered a genealogy in which the eighteenth-century literary public sphere informed the development of a public sphere of rational-critical debate that gave individuals in civil society a way to influence politics. He generally ignored religion in his historical account of the public sphere, as he has acknowledged.[14] And, until recently, religion did not figure in his further considerations on communicative action and the organization of modern society. So it is significant that Habermas in the last decade has begun to argue that finding ways to integrate religion into the public sphere is a vital challenge for contemporary society (and theories of contemporary society).[15] His work is appropriately a point of departure for the discussions in this book.

Habermas's argument is an elaboration of the fundamental premise that the public sphere of a democratic society must be open to all. It is imperative to include religious citizens both as a matter of fairness and as a matter of urgent practicality. Religiously informed actors, including Christian fundamentalists in America and Islamists in Europe, matter so much in contemporary political life that we endanger the future of the democratic polity if we cannot integrate them into the workings of public reason. Further, Habermas sees political liberalism as in need of new moral insights and commitments and recognizes religion as a potential source of renewal. Such renewal should not take the form of a direct appeal to religious doctrines or comprehensive worldviews in ways that foreclose public debate. His opening examination of Carl Schmitt's political theology is precisely an attempt to put to rest the notion that political authority can derive either directly from religious revelation or from the self-founding sovereignty of an absolutist state. Insisting on a homogeneous mass society as the basis for the constitutional state, and relying on the shifting moods of such a society for political motivation, can only in the most superficial sense be seen as involving democracy. Schmitt's approach is both impossible, because society has become irretrievably pluralist, and directly authoritarian despite its democratic disguise. Political religion could have similar implications. What prevents this is commitment to public reason—and on this Habermas is in accord with Neuhaus. Religious and nonreligious citizens meet as equals, and religious ideas inform the public sphere through argument rather than through simply dissemination (let alone top-down authority).

Because the public sphere is for Habermas a realm of rational-critical argumentation and propositional content, admission is a matter of ability and willingness to participate in open debate. He worries that religious commitments inhibit this, both because faith or revelation are reasons that can't hold weight for those who don't experience them and because religious ideas come in language that is not accessible to those outside particular traditions. Accordingly, he calls for the potential truth contents religious people bring to public discourse to be "translated" so that they are stated in ways not dependent on specifically religious sources. Translation should not be a burden only on religious citizens, but an ethical obligation for non-religious citizens who should seek to understand what is said on religious grounds as best they can. But not all that religious citizens have to say is "translatable"; the residuum can be allowed in informal public discourse, but an institutional filter must exist to keep it out of the formal deliberations of political bodies.

Habermas's arguments leave the worries that the translation proviso is necessarily asymmetrical and that the call to recognize explicitly religious voices in the public sphere is at least partially instrumental—a call to include ideas because they are useful while implicitly doubting that they may be true.

Charles Taylor's approach speaks to each of these worries. Taylor approaches religion in the public sphere indirectly, as it were, through competing meanings of secularism. He has addressed other dimensions of the topic in *A Secular Age*. Here his focus is specifically on what sort of stance toward religion is required of a modern democratic state with a diverse population. He agrees with the notion that states must achieve neutrality, but sees two problems with most discussion. First, there is the tendency to fixate on religion, as though it posed radically different questions from all other sorts of differences among citizens. It doesn't, suggests Taylor. And the issue is not just a misunderstanding of religion but also a misunderstanding of the relationship of both culture and personal agency to public reason. Deep differences requiring translation—and perhaps further work to reach common understandings—are not limited to religious differences. Reason is always rooted in culture, experience, and what Taylor has called "strong horizons of evaluation" (that citizens seldom make fully explicit in either public reason or their own private reflections). "The point of state neutrality," he writes, "is precisely to avoid favoring or disfavoring not just religious positions, but any basic position, religious or nonreligious."

Taylor's second point follows from this. Given the importance and variations of deep commitments that orient citizens, there is no solution to be found by means of an institutional arrangement demarcating where deep values may be asserted and where they may not. At best, formulae like "the separation of church and state" are shorthand heuristics. But much more important for democratic societies is exploring ways to work for common goals—like liberty, equality, and fraternity. Constructing a democratic life together may depend more on being able to engage in such shared positive pursuits than on any institutional arrangement (or, indeed, agreement on all the reasons to engage in common pursuits). This also suggests that we should not understand the public sphere entirely in terms of argumentation about the truth value of propositions. It is a realm of creativity and social imaginaries in which citizens give shared form to their lives together, a realm of exploration, experiment, and partial agreements. Citizens need to find ways to treat each other's basic commitments with respect; fortunately they are also likely to find considerable overlaps in what they value.

Like Habermas, Taylor is concerned with identifying ways in which the public sphere can help to produce greater integration among citizens who enter public discourse with different views. Habermas stresses agreement and clearer knowledge while Taylor stresses mutual recognition and collaboration in common pursuits. But both see excluding religion from the public sphere as undermining the solidarity and creativity they seek. In different ways, Judith Butler and Cornel West ask about the limits of optimistic visions of the public sphere in which harmonious integration is the apparent telos.

Butler emphasizes occasions when it is impossible to achieve intellectual (or political) integration, including agreement on truth and value. Religious sources of ethical insight may matter enormously precisely when deliberation in the public sphere fails. Deep differences may remain—and remain troubling and troubled. Religion may provide a guide to action in the face of divisions it cannot undo. This is true especially when the realities of state power and geopolitics bring people into the same place, not necessarily by choice, and into social relationships, though they do not understand themselves to constitute a single people or polity. Pluralization is not always a challenge to be overcome.

Butler offers the idea of cohabitation as an alternative, or perhaps a crucial supplement, to that of integrative public reason. It is an understanding of what is both possible and ethically right that she draws from Jewish tradition, shaped by the historical experience of statelessness, subjection, and partial autonomy under states Jews did not control. The ethic of cohabitation thus has an internal relationship to being Jewish—and on this basis criticizing state violence that is at odds with cohabitation must be "a Jewish thing to do." Butler sees this as more than simply distinguishing "progressive" Jewish positions from others, because it entails taking seriously the limits of any identitarian concept of Jewishness—of identifying Jews with a nation-unto-itself in the manner of much nationalist rhetoric rather than with the position of people always already engaged in relationship with non-Jews.

Cohabitation guides an ethics on which Jews should act independently of whether it is met by a symmetrical commitment on the part of non-Jews, though they may hope that it will be. It is thus a religious contribution to the public sphere that does not depend on agreement but applies in its absence. Its significance comes from underwriting recognition of the importance or at least inevitability of continued life in the same place, even when values, identities, and practices cannot readily be reconciled. It is an understanding of what is materially necessary and an ethics following from this that does not depend on theory or discourses of justice—and may even be impeded by the attempt to ground all action in resolution of claims to justice. Taking cohabitation seriously indicts attempts to base politics exclusively on consensus, even when this is approached as a matter of the most inclusive possible public reason.

Cornel West, blues man in the life of the mind, jazzman in the world of ideas, challenges conceptions of public life limited to rational arguments, ethical consensus, and even cultural harmony. The secular need to hear the music of religion, he says, but also vice versa. Mutual understanding is achieved through empathy and imagination, learning the rhythm of each other's dances and the tunes of each other's songs. This sort of knowledge is tested in action, not in propositions; the capacity to understand each other is not derived from arguments. Of course, this partially prediscursive ability to understand each other may be the condition of good arguments in which participants feel they make progress toward knowledge.

West hopes for reconciliation and mutual understanding, but he doesn't see religion offering this in a neat package. In the first place, he joins the others in this book in suggesting that we live in a multiplicity of different intellectual, cultural, and religious frameworks. We are called to find ways to relate well to each other, ideally to understand each other, but not to erase these differences. Indeed, participation in the public sphere offers not just collective benefits but also the personal good of existence enriched by greater ability to put oneself in the shoes of others. This is not simply an instrumental good conducive to potential agreement; it is valuable in itself. More than this, West insists that the Christian message (at least, and he doesn't rule out similar messages from other traditions) is not simply a logic of equivalence—Rawlsian justice—but of a superabundance of love. Justice would be good, I think he is saying. It would be a big improvement. We should feel "righteous indignation against injustice." But in itself justice cannot be entirely definitive of the good.

Perhaps most important, West calls on us to find resources within our traditions, including especially our various religious traditions, to disrupt harmonies that disguise underlying discord. He calls on us to bear witness to suffering (even when we do not yet know how to end it). He insists that prophetic religion has a place in the public sphere, for its very disruptions are calls to attention that make people see realities that make them uncomfortable. Calls to attention are not arguments or propositions that should be subjected to critique; they are performances of a different sort. Prophetic religion is neither consensus building nor simply dissent; it is a challenge to think and look and even smell (funky) anew; it is not a matter of gradual evolutionary progress but of urgency. The demand prophecy makes on us is not that of faith but that of truth—or, rather, potential truth, for the prophet articulates not only the evils at hand but the possibilities of a future in which we are damned for what we have done and a future in which we have the chance to do better.

To say that religion has power in the public sphere is not to say that it can be easily absorbed or that it should be. It is a basis for radical challenges and radical questions; it brings enthusiasm, passion, indignation, outrage, and love. If enthusiasm is sometimes harnessed to unreflective conviction, passion is also vital to critical engagement with existing institutions and dangerous trends. The public sphere and the practice of public reason have power too. And they not only take from religion but also offer it opportunities to advance by reflection and critical argument.

The public sphere is a realm of rational-critical debate in which matters of the public good are considered. It is also a realm of cultural formation in which argument is not the only important practice and creativity and ritual, celebration and recognition are all important. It includes the articulation between deep sensibilities and explicit understandings and it includes the effort—aided sometimes by prophetic calls to attention—to make the way we think and act correspond to our deepest values or moral commitments.

NOTES

1. Cited from Leslie Hazleton, *After the Prophet* (New York: Doubleday, 2009; Kindle edition).

2. Michael Young, *Bearing Witness Against Sin: The Evangelical Birth of the American Social Movement* (Chicago: University of Chicago Press, 2007).

3. Walter Rauschenbusch, *Christianity and the Social Crisis* (New York: Macmillan, 1907), pp. 48–49.

4. Quoted from Paul Johnson, *Modern Times* (New York: Harper, 1983), p. 209.

5. See John Rawls, *A Brief Inquiry Into the Meaning of Sin and Faith: With "On My Religion"* (Cambridge: Harvard University Press, 2009).

6. Charles Taylor, *A Secular Age* (Cambridge: Harvard University Press, 2007).

7. Richard John Neuhaus, *The Naked Public Sphere* (Grand Rapids: Erdmans, 1984).

8. Op cit., p. 36.

9. David Sorkin, *The Religious Enlightenment* (Princeton: Princeton University Press, 2008).

10. Joachim Israel, *The Radical Enlightenment* (Oxford: Oxford University Press, 2001).

11. David Zaret, *The Origins of Democratic Culture: Printing, Petitions, and the Public Sphere in Early Modern England* (Princeton: Princeton University Press, 1999).

12. A. Benchimol, "Cultural Historiography and the Scottish Enlightenment Public Sphere: Placing Habermas in Eighteenth-Century Edinburgh," in A. Benchimol and W. Maley, eds., *Spheres of Influence: Intellectual and Cultural Publics from Shakespeare to Habermas* (Bern: Lang, 2007), pp. 105–150.

13. Jürgen Habermas, *Structural Transformation of the Public Sphere* (Cambridge: MIT Press, 1989). Since people sometimes obsess over terminology, it is worth noting that though the term public sphere (*sphäre*) was

considered in the original German, the title and most of the text focused on "publicness" (*öffentlichkeit*); the French translation was *L'espace public*.

14. See Jürgen Habermas, "Further Reflections on the Public Sphere," in Craig Calhoun, ed., *Habermas and the Public Sphere* (Cambridge: MIT Press, 1992).

15. See especially essays gathered in Jürgen Habermas, *Between Naturalism and Religion* (Cambridge: MIT Press, 2008).

INDEX

Adorno, Theodor, 103
Agamben, Giorgio, 16
Aquinas, Thomas, 62
Arendt, Hannah, 16, 45, 80, 81,
    85, 87; *Eichmann in Jerusalem,*
    83, 84; political Zionism, 77, 79,
    82; statelessness/exile, 78, 86
Aristotle, 45, 120
Atatürk, Mustafa Kemal, 37

Badiou, Alain, 108
Beckett, Samuel, 98, 99
Beethoven, Ludwig van, 93
Benjamin, Walter, 88, 102, 103,
    112, history, 84, 88, "Theses
    'On the Concept of History,'"
    81, 82, 83
Bhargava, Rajeev, 35

Bloch, Ernst, 107
Briand, Aristide, 40
Bryan, William Jennings, 121
Buber, Martin, 77, 78
Butler, Judith, 7, 8; cohabitation, 9,
    130

Calhoun, Craig, 12
Casanova, José, 36
Chekhov, Anton, 98, 99
Churchill, Winston, 108
Connolly, William, 85
Conrad, Joseph, 105
Cortés, Donoso, 22
Coughlin, Father, 124

Darwin, Charles, 94
De Bonald, Louis, 22

De Condorcet, Marquis, 55, 56
De Maistre, Joseph, 22
Derrida, Jacques, 16, 96
Descartes, Rene, 55
Dewey, John, 121, 122, 124
Durkheim, Emile, 105

Ellison, Ralph Waldo, 98

Falwell, Jerry, 125
Fanon, Frantz, 96
Ferry, Jules, 40
Friedman, Thomas, 104

Gandhi, Mahatma, 116
Gauchet, Marcel, 39
Goethe, Johann Wolfgang, 93

Habermas, Jürgen, 54, 118; the
    political, 5, 16, 17, 18, 46;
    public reason, 49, 50, 53; the
    public sphere, 127, 128;
    *Structural Transformation of
    the Public Sphere*, 2, 3, 4, 126
Hayes, Isaac, 104
Heschel, Rabbi Abraham Joshua,
    95
Hitchens, Christopher, 93
Hitler, Adolf, 108
Hobbes, Thomas, 19, 47, 56
Holiday, Billie, 98
Homer, 93
Hume, David, 55

Israel, Joachim, 125

James, William, 94
Jaspers, Karl, 94
Jaurés, Jean, 40
Jefferson, Thomas, 98

Kafka, Franz, 81, 98, 99, 103
Kant, Immanuel, 40, 50, 53,
    64, 85
King, B. B., 98
King, Martin Luther, 63, 65, 95,
    100, 108, 122
Krugman, Paul, 97

Laclau, Ernesto, 16
Lefort, Claude, 16, 27, 47
Lilla, Mark, 51
Locke, John, 47
Luria, Isaac, 80

McCarthy, Thomas, 92
Marcuse, Herbert, 103
Marx, Karl, 50, 64
Meerpol, Abel, 98
Metz, Johann Baptist, 28
Morrison, Toni, 98

Nancy, Jean-Luc, 16
Neuhaus, Richard John, 124, 125,
    127

Obama, Barack, 97, 99, 100, 104

Pilate, Pontius, 106
Piterberg, Gabriel, 81
Plato, 93, 95

Rauschenbusch, Walter, 121
Rawls, John, 37, 50; political
    liberalism, 11, 19, 23; public
    reason, 35, 49, 53, 115;
    religion in the public sphere,
    4, 6, 24
Raz-Krakotzin, Amnon, 81
Renouvier, Charles Bernard,
    39
Ricoeur, Paul, 96
Rorty, Richard, 11
Rosenzweig, Franz, 77
Rousseau, Jean-Jacques, 47

Said, Edward, 77, 78, 79, 84
Santayana, George, 94
Schiller, Friedrich, 103

Schmitt, Carl, 27, 127, liberalism,
    21, 22, the political 16, 19, 20,
    23
Scholem, Gershom, 77, 80, 81, 82,
    99
Sharyati, Ali, 118
Shelley, Percy Bysshe, 93, 96, 97
Socrates, 9
Sophocles, 98
Story, Joseph, 38
Strauss, Leo, 2, 16

Taylor, Charles, 6, 7, 92, 129; A
    Secular Age, 5, 128

Unger, Roberto, 92

Weber, Max, 105
West, Cornel, 9, 10, 11
West, Nathanael, 94, 131, 132
Wolin, Sheldon, 99